Wildlife Population and Harvest Trends in the United States

A Technical Document Supporting
the Forest Service 2010 RPA Assessment

Curtis H. Flather, Michael S. Knowles,
Martin F. Jones, and Carol Schilli

Flather, Curtis H.; Knowles, Michael S.; Jones, Martin F.; Schilli, Carol. 2013. **Wildlife population and harvest trends in the United States: A technical document supporting the Forest Service 2010 RPA Assessment.** Gen. Tech. Rep. RMRS-GTR-296. Fort Collins, CO: U.S. Department of Agriculture, Forest Service, Rocky Mountain Research Station. 94 p.

Abstract: The Forest and Rangeland Renewable Resources Planning Act (RPA) of 1974 requires periodic assessments of the condition and trends of the nation's renewable natural resources. Data from many sources were used to document recent historical trends in big game, small game, migratory game birds, furbearers, nongame, and imperiled species. Big game and waterfowl have generally increased in population and harvest trends. Many small upland and webless migratory game bird species have declined notably in population or harvest. Considerable declines in fur harvest since the 2000 RPA Assessment have occurred. Among the 426 breeding bird species with sufficient data to estimate nationwide trends, 45 percent had stable abundance since the mid-1960s; however, more species declined (31 percent) than increased (24 percent). A total of 1,368 bird species were formally listed as threatened or endangered under the Endangered Species Act—a net gain of 278 species since the 2000 RPA Assessment. Most forest bird communities are expected to support a lower variety of species. America's wildlife resources will continue to be pressured by diverse demands for ecosystem services from humans. Collaborative planning and management among private and public land owners, and which spans the research and management branches of the Forest Service, will be vital to conserving and sustaining the nation's wildlife resources.

Authors

Curtis H. Flather is a research ecologist and **Michael S. Knowles** is an ecologist—both are with the U.S. Forest Service, Rocky Mountain Research Station in Fort Collins, CO.

Martin F. Jones is a senior research associate and technical writer and **Carol Schilli** is a research associate and data analyst—both are with Responsive Management in Harrisonburg, VA.

You may order additional copies of this publication by sending your mailing information in label form through one of the following media. Please specify the publication title and number.

Publishing Services

Telephone	(970) 498-1392
FAX	(970) 498-1122
E-mail	rschneider@fs.fed.us
Web site	http://www.fs fed.us/rmrs
Mailing Address	Publications Distribution
	Rocky Mountain Research Station
	240 West Prospect Road
	Fort Collins, CO 80526

Acknowledgments

This work was supported by the Forest Service Research and Development's RPA Assessment research program as part of the Forest Service's national assessment reporting requirements mandated by the Forest and Rangeland Renewable Resources Planning Act. We wish to thank Ron Regan, Executive Director, Association of Fish and Wildlife Agencies, for coordinating requests to state wildlife agencies; Bryant White, Association of Fish and Wildlife Agencies, for compiling and providing data on fur resources; Jason McNees, Conservation Data Analyst, NatureServe for assisting in the compilation of threatened and endangered species and at-risk species data; John R. Sauer, U.S. Geological Survey, Biological Resources Division, Patuxent Wildlife Research Center for completing trend analyses for breeding birds throughout the continental United States; Laura Ellison, U.S. Geological Survey, Biological Resources Division, Fort Collins Science Center, for sharing her trend analyses of bat colonies; and all the state and federal biologists who cooperated in this national effort to compile data on the population and harvest of wildlife resources. This report also benefited from the constructive comments we received from Dr. William Ripple (Professor, Oregon State University), Thomas Franklin (Senior Director of Science and Policy, Theodore Roosevelt Conservation Partnership), Ron Regan (Executive Director, Association of Fish and Wildlife Agencies), Priya Nanjappa (Amphibian and Reptile Coordinator, Association of Fish and Wildlife Agencies), and Dr. Linda Langner (RPA Assessment National Program Leader, U.S. Forest Service).

Contents

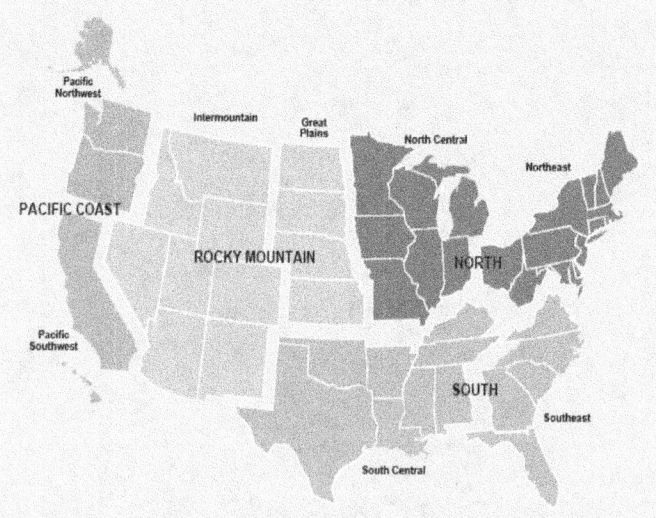

Introduction _____

The United States encompasses some 9.8 million km^2 of which 93 percent is land and 7 percent is classified as inland or coastal waters (USDA, Forest Service 2012a). The ecosystems that compose this land and water base support a rich diversity of terrestrial and aquatic species (Ricketts and others 1999) from which the American public derives substantial ecosystem services (Millennium Ecosystem Assessment 2005). The societal benefits attributed to the species inhabiting these ecosystems are many and include the provision of food, recreational opportunities, spiritual fulfillment, intellectual stimulation, and maintenance of important ecosystem functions (Daily 1997; Pimentel and others 1997; Fisher and others 2009). The realization of these ecosystem services is not a given but is affected by ecosystem conditions, which are becoming predominantly driven by human activities (Kareiva and Marvier 2011). Growing human populations, land use conversions, and intensive uses of natural resources are raising concerns that the ability of ecosystems to provide these services sustainably may be compromised (Balmfort and Bond 2005).

Given the degree to which humans can affect ecosystems (Vitousek and others 1997; Naeem and others 2012), it is important to assess the consequences of ecosystem change to natural resources and human well-being (Herrick and others 2010; Raudsepp-Hearne and Capistrano 2010; Kareiva and Marvier 2011) across broad geographic scales if resource management and policy decisions are to remain science based (Schimel 2011). The need to assess the resource consequences associated with human use and management of ecosystems as a check against ecosystem degradation was actually anticipated nearly four decades ago with passage of the Forest and Rangeland Renewable Resources Planning Act (RPA) of 1974 (P.L. 93-378, 88 Stat 475, as amended). This legislation requires the U.S. Forest Service to prepare periodic resource assessments on the nation's forest and range lands that report on (1) the current status and condition of resources based on an analysis of recent historic trends and (2) the future resource situation based on projections derived from a set of basic assumptions that define the demographic, socioeconomic, energy use, and climate change context within which resource supply and demands interact (Cortner and Schwitzer 1981; USDA, Forest Service 2012a). Moreover, it warrants emphasis that these assessments are to address resource status and trends on all lands, not just lands directly administered by the U.S. Forest Service, and for which the agency has main jurisdiction over resource stewardship decisions.

The primary objective of this report is to present recent historical trends in the population and harvests of wildlife species across the United States as one set of indicators that reflect resource condition as required by the RPA. We also review some of the implications of these trends for the long term management of wildlife resources with particular emphasis on the three main programs in the USDA, Forest Service—namely, the National Forest System, State and Private Forestry, and Research and Development. For the purposes of this report, "wildlife" is defined as unconfined and undomesticated vertebrate and invertebrate species that primarily inhabit terrestrial ecosystems. Trends associated with species that are primarily associated with aquatic habitats are covered in a companion report (Loftus and Flather 2012). The trends reviewed herein update wildlife resource trends that have been presented as components of previous RPA Assessment reporting cycles (see USDA, Forest Service 1981; Flather and Hoekstra 1989; Flather and others 1999; Flather and others 2008; Flather and others 2009a) and provide an opportunity for evaluating the degree to which past trajectories have remained the same or changed. Although our definition of wildlife (see glossary in Appendix A) extends beyond the traditional focus on species that can be legally harvested, available data do carry with them a legacy of taxonomic bias that can be traced to the recreational and commercial importance of certain species and species groups. Although we admit these biases exist in the available data, we must emphasize that our intent is to review trends in wildlife resources across a set of species that will be broadly reflective of wildlife species writ large.[1]

Methods

Owing to the variety of species that inhabit the United States and the absence of truly comprehensive data on the distribution and abundance of species, the methods used here to document population and harvest trends were equally varied. Moreover, our treatment of species trends will be taxonomically uneven given that monitoring efforts have tended to focus on vertebrates. Even among vertebrate groups, there is differential emphasis placed on those species that are harvested, important to wildlife viewing recreation, or are of conservation concern because their rarity has elevated the possibility of extinction and the potential to erode key ecological processes that affect the provisioning of services that humans derive from ecosystems (Chapin and others 2000; Flather and Sieg 2007; Ehrlich and Pringle 2008).

For these reasons, the data compiled here are derived from a number of sources—each with its own strengths and limitations. Some sources support stronger inferences about the direction and magnitude of distributional or abundance changes than others. It is our intent to highlight those strengths and weaknesses so that readers can appropriately judge the underlying uncertainty in the data, and to make recommendations that could mitigate noted limitations in existing wildlife resource monitoring programs. Before reviewing the data sources that formed the basis for this assessment, we first highlight the species groups and geographic partitions that will serve to organize our review of wildlife population and harvest trends.

Species Groups and Regional Definitions

Because of the diversity of resident and common migrant species that occur within the United States, we address the status and trends of wildlife by major species categories including: (1) those commonly harvested for recreation, subsistence, or commercial gain (i.e., big game, small game, migratory game birds, and furbearers); (2) those not typically harvested but having high public interest (i.e., breeding birds, amphibians, bats, and pollinators); and (3) those that have been determined by formal population assessment to have extinction risks that warrant elevated conservation focus (i.e., imperiled species).

Where data structure and availability permit, we supplement national trends among species that make up these major species categories with RPA regional trends. Each region is composed of multiple states that have been defined by the Forest Service for strategic

---

[1] The scientific name for species mentioned in this report can be found in Appendix B.

resource planning purposes. These are the North, South, Rocky Mountain, and Pacific Coast Assessment regions (Figure 1). We were unable to re-aggregate base data into the RPA regions for some species groups. In these instances we report subnational trends for other geographic regions when they are well established in wildlife monitoring and planning. Table 1 identifies the geographic reporting units that were supported by the data for each species group.

Data Sources and Species Group Analyses

The trends reported were compiled from several sources, including cooperating state wildlife agencies, federal wildlife management and research agencies, and nongovernmental organizations that maintain comprehensive data on the status of U.S. biodiversity. Because data sources vary by species categories, the details concerning source documents and databases will be described separately for each species category. We provide a summary of data sources by species category in Table 1. Given the diversity of data sources, it should not be surprising that data quality also varied greatly. In some cases, national inventories have been designed to provide statistically based estimates from which strong inferences on population size and trend can be made at state, regional, and national scales. In other cases the estimates were based on the best judgments of wildlife professionals, and more emphasis should be placed on the direction of the trend rather than the actual magnitude of the estimates.

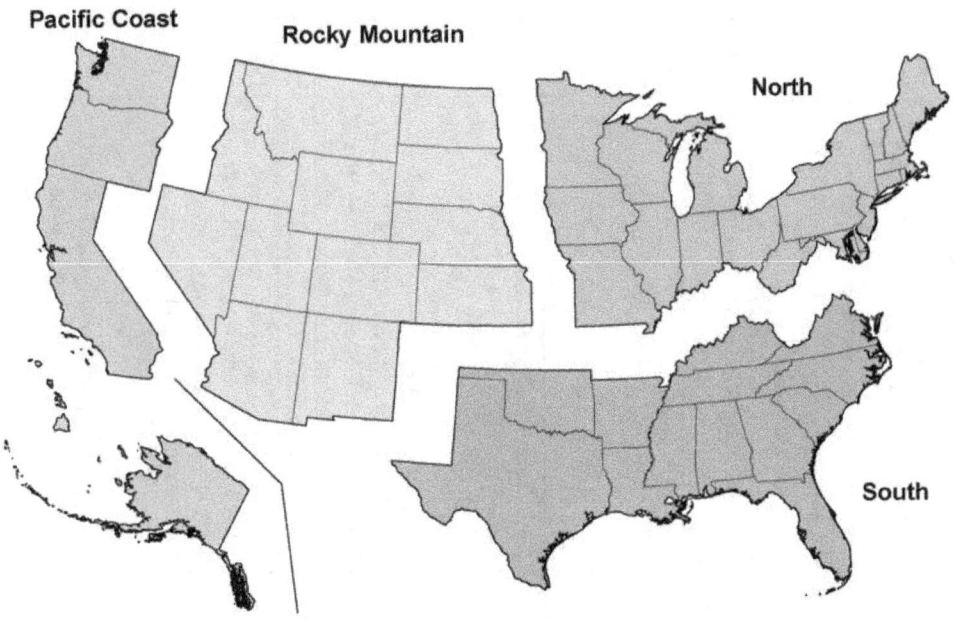

Figure 1—Forest Service RPA Assessment regions.

Table 1—Data sources used to describe the current status and recent historical trend of wildlife species groups.

Species Group	Data Sources	Comments	Geographic Reporting Units
Big and Small Game	State Wildlife Agencies	Data acquired with the assistance of the Association of Fish and Wildlife Agencies and Responsive Management. Requests were sent to all 50 state wildlife agencies to review the accuracy of **population** and **harvest** estimates for recreationally important big and small game species. Data were provided to the state agencies with estimates from 1975 to 2000, in 5-year intervals, with requests to confirm historical entries and provide recent estimates of harvest and population levels for 2005 and 2008.	National; RPA regions
	John Sauer, personal communication, U.S. Geological Survey, Biological Resources Division, Patuxent Wildlife Research Center, 2010	**Population** trend estimates for upland game birds as indexed by relative abundance were based on the North American Breeding Bird Survey data.	National; RPA regions
Migratory Game Birds			
Ducks	USDI, Fish and Wildlife Service (2010)	Total duck **population** estimates from 1955-2010. Includes mallards*, gadwall*, American wigeon*, green-winged teal*, blue-winged teal*, northern shoveler*, northern pintail*, redhead*, canvasback*, scaup*, American black duck, ring-necked duck, goldeneyes, bufflehead, and ruddy duck. Excludes scoters, eiders, long-tailed ducks, mergansers and wood ducks. The current (2010) population estimates for the 10 principal duck species, indicated with a asterisk (*) above.	National
	U. S. Fish and Wildlife Service, Environment Canada, and Secretario of Desarrollo Social Mexico (1994)	Continental **population goals** for ducks were obtained from the 1994 Update to the North American Waterfowl Management Plan.	National
	Kathy Fleming, personal communication, U.S. Department of the Interior, U.S. Fish and Wildlife Service, Division of Migratory Bird Management, Branch of Population and Habitat Assessment, Laurel, MD. 10 Jan 2011		
	Robert Raftovich, personal communication, U.S. Department of the Interior, U.S. Fish and Wildlife Service, Division of Migratory Bird Management, Branch of Harvest Surveys, Laurel, MD 23 Jul 2009	Despite a change in methodology in 1999 to the Harvest Information Program (HIP), duck **harvest** estimates are consistent enough to combine with data used from the 2000 RPA Assessment.	National; Administrative flyways
	Paul Padding, personal communication, U.S. Department of the Interior, U.S. Fish and Wildlife Service, Office of Migratory Bird Management, Laurel, MD. 29 May 1996		

(continued)

Table 1—(Continued).

Species Group	Data Sources	Comments	Geographic Reporting Units
Geese	USDI, Fish and Wildlife Service (2010)	North American Canada goose population estimates for the 1970-2010 period. The time period for the Atlantic Flyway Resident Population is short relative to time periods for other populations because the survey changed how birds observed as singles, and as pairs, were treated.	Managed populations
	Tim Moser, personal communication, U.S. Department of the Interior, Fish and Wildlife Service, Division of Migratory Bird Management, Laurel, MD. 20 Jan 2011	The population indices for the Mississippi Flyway Giant Population/ Resident Population (MFGP/MFRP) since 1992/93 were those obtained during the spring in the Mississippi Flyway States/Provinces. Those used in the 2000 RPA Assessment (1969-1995) were winter estimates obtained during mid-December or early January. The two methods are not comparable so we only show the results from the spring surveys.	Managed populations
	Robert Raftovich, personal communication, U.S. Department of the Interior, U.S. Fish and Wildlife Service, Division of Migratory Bird Management, Branch of Harvest Surveys, Laurel, MD. 23 Jul 2009	Despite a change in methodology in 1999 to the Harvest Information Program (HIP), goose harvest estimates are consistent enough to combine with data used from the 2000 RPA Assessment.	National; Administrative flyway
	Paul Padding, personal communication, U.S. Department of the Interior, Fish and Wildlife Service, Office of Migratory Bird Management, Laurel, MD, 29 May 1996		
Swans	USDI, Fish and Wildlife Service (2010)	The different time series for the Western (1970-2010) and Eastern (1982-2010) swan populations is based on revisions to the 2007 Management Plan for the Eastern swan population. Those changes to the population survey prevented us from reporting pre-1982 population indices.	Managed populations
	Mark Koneff, personal communication, U.S. Department of the Interior, Fish and Wildlife Service, Division of Migratory Bird Management, Laurel, MD. 4 Aug 2009		
	Tim Moser, personal communication, U.S. Department of the Interior, Fish and Wildlife Service, Division of Migratory Bird Management, Laurel, MD. 10 Aug 2009		
	Robert Raftovich, personal communication, U.S. Department of the Interior, Fish and Wildlife Service, Division of Migratory Bird Management, Branch of Harvest Surveys, Laurel, MD. 23 Jul 2009	Swan harvest estimates, 1962-2007.	National; Managed populations
Mourning Dove	Sanders, Todd, personal communication, U.S. Department of the Interior, Fish and Wildlife Service, Division of Migratory Bird Management, Laurel, MD. 4 Jan 2011	Because doves are managed by Management Unit, their population estimates generally are not reported at the national level. National band data appropriate to the 2003-2009 period were provided.	National

(continued)

Table 1—(Continued).

Species Group	Data Sources	Comments	Geographic Reporting Units
	Sanders and Parker (2010)	Population indices for the 1966-2010 period.	Management units
	Padding and others (2005); U.S. Fish and Wildlife Service (2006a,b; 2007a,b); Raftovich and others (2009); Raftovich and others (2010)	Harvest data used here differ from the 2000 RPA Assessment because of the implementation of the Harvest Information Program (HIP) in 1999. HIP survey estimates of dove harvest have been available since 1999. Although estimates from 1999-2002 should be considered preliminary, as refinements are still being made in the sampling frame and estimation techniques.	National; Management units
Woodcock	Cooper and Parker (2010)	Population indices for the 1968-2010 period.	National; Management regions
	Kelley (2002, 2003, 2004); Kelley and Rau (2005, 2006); Kelley and others (2007); Cooper and others (2008); Cooper and Parker (2009, 2010)	Harvest data used here differ from the 2000 RPA Assessment because of the implementation of the Harvest Information Program (HIP) in 1999. HIP survey estimates of woodcock harvest have been available since 1999. Although estimates from 1999-2002 have been finalized, the estimates from 2003-2009 should be considered preliminary, as refinements are still being made in the sampling frame and estimation techniques.	National; Management regions
Furbearers	Association of Fish and Wildlife Agencies (2010)	Fur harvest was compiled by the U.S. Furbearer Conservation Technical Work Group of the Association of Fish and Wildlife Agencies in conjunction with the assistance of state wildlife agencies.	National; RPA regions
Nongame			
Breeding Birds	John Sauer, personal communication, U.S. Geological Survey, Biological Resources Division, Patuxent Wildlife Research Center, Laurel, MD. 4 Jun 2010	Population trend estimates for 426 breeding birds as indexed by relative abundance were based on the North American Breeding Bird Survey (BBS) data.	National; RPA regions
	USGS Patuxent Wildlife Research Center. 2009. North American Breeding Bird Survey ftp data set, version 2009.1 (ftp://ftpext.usgs. gov/pub/er/md/laurel/BBS/Archive files/Version 2009v1/[accessed: 9 June 2010])	Forest bird species richness was calculated by (1) extracting forest-associated species from the Breeding Bird Survey data for each survey route; (2) running the route-level data through COMDYN (http://www.mbr-pwrc. usgs.gov/software/) which computed estimates of species richness; and (3) using ESRI's ArcMap software to map the COMDYN species richness estimates using the inverse distance weighting interpolation method.	National; Isopleth map of forest bird richness
Amphibians	NatureServe (2011)	Using data provided from NatureServe's Central databases (NatureServe 2011) we tallied amphibian species of conservation concern according to NatureServe's global conservation status ranks. Species of concern were based on ranks of presumed extinct (GX), possibly extinct (GH), critically imperiled (G1), imperiled (G2), and vulnerable (G3).	National; RPA regions

(continued)

Table 1—(Continued).

Species Group	Data Sources	Comments	Geographic Reporting Units
	Amphibian Research and Monitoring Initiative (Adams and others 2012)	Trends in amphibian species **occupancy** from 118 time series collected over 39 monitoring areas distributed across the coterminous United States.	National
Bats	Ellison and others (2003)	Estimates of **colony size** at winter and summer roost sites.	RPA regions
	Bat Conservation International (http://www.batcon.org)	The map documents counties with confirmed or suspected **cases of white-nose syndrome** from 2006/2007 to 2010/2011.	County
Pollinators	National Research Council (2007); Potts and others (2010); Cameron and others (2011)	Review of pollinator **population** status from various literature sources.	Global; Continental
	USGS Patuxent Wildlife Research Center. 2009. North American Breeding Bird Survey ftp data set, version 2009.1 (ftp://ftpext.usgs.gov/pub/er/md/laurel/BBS/Archive files/Version 2009v1/ [accessed: 9 June 2010])	**Population** trends of bird pollinators (hummingbirds) as indexed by relative abundance were based on North American Breeding Bird Survey data.	National; RPA regions
Imperiled Species	U.S. Department of the Interior, Fish and Wildlife Service, Endangered Species Bulletin (used prior to October 2009); and Listed species summary boxscore (used from October 2009 to present; http://ecos.fws.gov/tess_public/pub/boxScore.jsp)	Cumulative **number of species** formally listed as threatened or endangered by broad taxonomic groups.	National
	NatureServe (2010)	NatureServe's Central databases were queried for **counts of species,** within counties, that were formally listed as threatened or endangered or are considered to be at-risk of extinction according to NatureServe's conservation status ranks.	County
	NatureServe (2011)	NatureServe's Central databases were queried for **counts of species** by NatureServe's conservation status ranks. The percentage of total species that are considered to be at-risk of extinction or of conservation concern was reported.	National; RPA regions

Big and small game

The species that make up the big game category are among some of the most important in stimulating public concern for wildlife conservation (Organ and others 2010) and many of these species have long been highlighted as key wildlife management successes (Thomas 1990). Big game primarily includes large mammal species that are taken for sport or subsistence. Because of state agency convention, we also consider the wild turkey as a big game species. Data on big game populations and harvests were compiled primarily from cooperating state wildlife agencies. Supplemental long-term monitoring data from the North American Breeding Bird Survey was also used to evaluate national and regional wild turkey population trends (for details on our use of the Breeding Bird Survey, see the methods associated with *Nongame* wildlife).

Data queries designed to facilitate data entry by state wildlife agencies were developed cooperatively over the years with input from the U.S. Forest Service and the Natural Resources Conservation Service. Data entry requests to state wildlife agencies were coordinated through the Association of Fish and Wildlife Agencies, with follow-up requests to states facilitated by Responsive Management.[2] An electronic form for documenting population and harvest trends for selected species from 1975 through 2008 (in 5-year intervals except for the 3-year interval from 2005 to 2008) was provided to State Wildlife Directors along with data entry instructions. State biologists within each agency were asked to review historical estimates (acquired in previous RPA Assessment efforts) for accuracy, to provide estimates that were missing from the historical record, and to provide new estimates since the 2000 RPA Assessment (*cf.* Flather and others 1999) for 2005 and 2008 (some states provided estimates for 2007, 2009, or 2010 for the most recent estimate of population or harvest). Forms were returned electronically and entered into the RPA Wildlife database.[3] All states responded to our request for information.

We recognized at the outset that there were differences in the way that various states estimated population and harvest. Because of these interstate differences, we focused our interpretations on the trends in population and harvest rather than on the actual magnitude of the estimate for any particular time period. This strategy assumes that a consistent set of states can provide estimates for each 5-year reporting period and that within-state procedures have remained comparable over the 1975-2008 period. A number of factors may cause state agency data to violate these assumptions. We highlight two of them here—data reporting gaps and changes to a State's procedures for estimating population or harvests—and we describe the methods that we used to minimize their impacts.

A lack of data for a particular species in a state can occur because of variation in the geographical distribution (i.e., that particular species' geographic range does not include that state, and, therefore, nothing will be reported), the species is not regularly harvested in that state, or because of an actual reporting gap in the data (i.e., that particular species' geographic

---

[2] Responsive Management is a research firm that conducts studies on the human dimensions of natural resources; information about the firm can be found at www.responsivemanagement.com.

[3] Data are available upon request from Michael S. Knowles (U.S. Forest Service, Rocky Mountain Research Station, Fort Collins, CO 80526, msknowles@fs fed.us).

range includes the state, the species is regularly harvested, but for whatever reason no data were reported). We identified all states with true data reporting gaps over the 1975-2008 period. Data gaps in the time series were filled by linear interpolation when estimates were available for adjacent 5-year time periods (that is, time periods prior to and after the data gap). Although there is a limitation in this procedure because it assumes a linear trend in population or harvest across the gap year, the procedure allows more states to be considered in the overall analysis. Maximizing the number of states that contribute data helps ensure that the analysis of trends is not disproportionately influenced by data from one or a few states. When the data gap occurred at the terminal 2008 time period, we substituted 2007, 2009, or 2010 data when those were the only years for which the states could provide recent population or harvest estimates.

Changes to state agency procedures used to estimate harvests and/or populations were more problematic. We relied on state agency contacts to identify procedural changes that would affect comparability over time in the "comments" field in the electronic data entry form. In those identified cases, we examined state-specific trends to assess the effects of the procedural change on the interpretability of the trend over the 1975-2008 period. Discontinuities in trends were flagged, and we attempted to contact state agency biologists to determine if the harvest or population estimate could be made comparable over the time period. If the data could not be made comparable, then that particular state's data for that species were not included in the trend analysis. Note that the interpolation process previously described for data gaps was performed only on true data gaps and was not used in cases where a data gap was caused by our exclusion of data because of a lack of comparability within a state. In other words, when data were excluded because of procedural changes in estimating harvest or population, those gaps were not filled by interpolation based on the data before and after the gap; rather, they simply could not be included in the analysis of trends.

We report trends for a particular big game species only across those states that provided estimates (or for which data gaps could be filled) for the 1975 to 2008 period in 5-year intervals (with the exception of the last interval of 2005 to 2008). Previous RPA Assessments reported population and harvest trends for widespread (occurring in many states) species including black bear, deer (both white-tailed and mule deer combined), elk, pronghorn, and wild turkey. For this assessment we were able to generate separate population and harvest trends for white-tailed deer and mule deer. Even after implementing the above procedures to maximize the number of states contributing to national and regional trends, there were cases where some species had few states reporting data over the full 33-year period. Those trends that are based on only a few states should be interpreted with caution.

Species treated as small game typically share a number of attributes: they are small-bodied resident mammals or birds; they can be native or desired non-native species that were intentionally introduced to provide hunting opportunities; they are commonly associated with forest, grassland, arid land, and agricultural upland habitats; and they are hunted recreationally or for subsistence. Small game species pursued because of their commercial value are treated as furbearers—the status and trends of which are reviewed in a separate section. We compiled population and harvest statistics, as with big game, from cooperating state wildlife agencies. Because so few states were able to provide population estimates over the 1975-2008 period, we primarily relied on the Breeding Bird Survey to provide estimates of trends in relative abundance among resident upland game bird species (for details on our use of the Breeding Bird Survey, see the methods associated with *Nongame* wildlife) including northern bobwhite, mountain quail, scaled quail, California quail, Gambel's quail, blue grouse, ruffed grouse, greater prairie-chicken, sharp-tailed grouse, sage grouse, gray partridge, chukar, and ring-necked pheasant. In many cases, state wildlife agency data were not distinguishable to the species level. For this reason, most population and harvest trends from state agency data were reported for species groups that were taxonomically or ecologically similar. The species that compose these groups are defined in Table 2.

Table 2—Definition of small game species groups for reporting population and harvest trends.

Group name	Species
Cottontail	Species of the genus *Sylvilagus*
Hare	Species of the genus *Lepus*
Squirrel	Species of the genus *Sciurus* and red squirrel (*Tamiasciurus hudsonicus*)
Prairie grouse	Greater prairie-chicken (*Tympanuchus cupido*), lesser prairie-chicken (*Tympanuchus pallidicinctus*), sharp-tailed grouse (*Tympanuchus phasianellus*), and sage grouse (*Centrocercus urophasianus* and *C. minimus*)
Forest grouse	Ruffed grouse (*Bonasa umbellus*), spruce grouse (*Falcipennis canadensis*), and blue grouse (composed of dusky grouse [*Dendrapagus obscurus*] and sooty grouse [*Dendrapagus fuliginosus*])
Western quail	Montezuma quail (*Cyrtonyx montezumae*), scaled quail (*Callipepla squamata*), Gambel's quail (*Callipepla gambelii*), California quail (*Callipepla californica*), and mountain quail (*Oreortyx pictus*)

Migratory game birds

"Migratory game birds" refers to a collection of species, which include waterfowl (ducks, geese, and swans), and the so-called "webless" migratory species that include mourning dove and woodcock. Federal authority to conserve and manage migratory birds is rooted in a series of statutes that were passed in the early 1900s (Migratory Bird Act of 1913, Migratory Bird Treaty Act of 1918, Migratory Bird Conservation Act of 1929) and international agreements with Great Britain on behalf of Canada, as well as subsequent treaties established with Mexico (1936), Japan (1972), and the Soviet Union (1976) (Chandler 1985; Nichols and others 1995). The primary objective of the ongoing provisions of these treaties is the protection and conservation of migratory bird populations. Harvesting of migratory birds in a manner that is consistent with protection is a secondary objective. The long history of migratory bird management in North America that was initiated by these Acts and historic agreements has resulted in the development of, perhaps, the premier monitoring system for continentally distributed species in the world (Nichols and others 1995; Nichols and others 2007). Consequently, population and harvest estimates are among the most extensive (temporally and geographically) and the most reliable for resource planning.

Population and harvest trends and management objectives come primarily from annual reports published by the U.S. Fish and Wildlife Service and from the North American Waterfowl Plan (USDI, Fish and Wildlife Service and others 1994). Survey methodologies have changed for migratory birds since the 2000 RPA Assessment when estimates were based on questionnaires sent to hunters who purchased a federal duck stamp. Hunters who sought only webless migratory species were not required to purchase a duck stamp and, therefore, were not sampled, resulting in an underestimate for those species. The Harvest Information Program (HIP) was developed to address this issue and was designed to sample all hunters of migratory birds. Estimates from HIP have been available since 1999.

Furbearers

The term "furbearer" is used to group mammal species that have traditionally been trapped or harvested primarily for their fur (Organ and others 2001). The management of furbearer resources in the United States remains controversial, and efforts to restrict the harvest of furbearers have increased (Conover 2001). The nocturnal and secretive nature of many furbearers makes it difficult to evaluate the population status of most of these species. For this reason, we rely on harvest statistics as the only quantitative measure of status and trends for furbearers. Because variation in furbearer harvests is a complex interaction between population size, trapping effort, pelt prices, and the susceptibility of species to harvest (DeVink and others 2011), we recognize that harvest trends do not necessarily track population trends closely and are likely heavily influenced by pelt prices (see Flather and others 1999).

Fur harvest data from 1970 to 2008 were compiled by the U.S. Furbearer Conservation Technical Work Group of the Association of Fish and Wildlife Agencies with assistance from state wildlife agencies (Association of Fish and Wildlife Agencies 2010). Sources varied between agencies and years and included fur buyers, fur dealers, fur trapper reports, pelt tagging records, and questionnaires. Depending on each state's methodology, the totals may or may not include hunter harvest. For most species, the totals presented are largely trapper harvest and should be considered a minimum harvest.

Nongame

For our purposes, nongame species are defined as those species that are not consumptively taken for sport, subsistence, or profit. As such, nongame species constitute the overwhelming majority of species that are resident or seasonal inhabitants within the United States. Unfortunately, there are very few data sources available for most nongame species that would permit an exploration of national and regional population trends. One taxonomic group where sufficient population information does exist to support broad-scale analyses of abundance trends is birds.

We used the North American Breeding Bird Survey (BBS; http://www.mbr-pwrc.usgs.gov/bbs/bbs.html) to evaluate the status and trends among commonly occurring species throughout the United States. The BBS is an annual survey of more than 4,000 rural roadside routes, each 24.5 miles long, randomly located throughout the United States and Canada. Trained surveyors tally all birds seen or heard during a 3-minute period at 50 stops evenly spaced (half mile interval) along the route (for details on the BBS see Robbins and others 1986; Droege 1990). Counts of birds were used to evaluate trends in relative abundance of more than 400 species nationwide since 1966.

Trends were estimated using a log-linear hierarchical model that accounted for the serial (temporal) correlation among observations (Sauer and Link 2002). Trends were estimated route-by-route and then averaged among routes occurring in regions of interest. Differences in regional sampling coverage and survey quality are accounted for by weighting route data when estimating the average regional trend (see Link and Sauer 1994). Even though species population dynamics vary geographically (increasing in some areas while declining in others) and temporally (increasing over some periods of years and declining over others), the methods used here provide tenable summaries of large-scale patterns of bird population change (Sauer and Link 2002:1750).

Trends were estimated over two broad periods of time: long-term trends were estimated over the 1966–2008 period and short-term trends were estimated over the 1996–2008 period to assess the degree to which bird trends have changed from the previous RPA Assessment (cf. Flather and others 1999). To qualify for analysis, each bird species had to have been detected on at least 15 routes. We counted species as having an increasing or decreasing trend if the slope of the regression differed from zero with probability $P<0.05$ in a positive or negative direction, respectively. Regression slopes that were not significantly different from zero were counted as stable.

Relative abundance trends for each species were summarized in two ways. First, we estimated the number of species with statistically significant increasing, decreasing, or stable trends nationwide and for each RPA region. Second, to provide a more detailed accounting of how birds with different ecologies have responded to changes in the environment, we grouped birds according to life-history characteristics, including nest type/location (cavity, open cup, ground or low, midstory or canopy), migration status (neotropical migrant, short-distance migrant, permanent resident), and breeding habitat affinity (woodland, shrubland, grassland, wetland or open water, urban) according to the classification of Peterjohn and Sauer (1993), and then we analyzed each life-history group. Specifically, the number of species with increasing, decreasing, or stable trends was estimated separately for each life-history group. To compare the pattern of breeding bird trends among life-history groups and among RPA regions, we estimated weighted means of the percentage of birds with increasing or decreasing trends by using the number of species within each group that occurred in a particular RPA region as the weights.

Because we tested for slope deviations from zero across many species, there is a legitimate concern that some significant trends could be observed solely due to chance (Benjamini and Hochberg 1995). Although methodologies exist to reduce such errors, their implementation increases the chance that a species undergoing a true population increase or decline will be missed (Perneger 1998; Nakagawa 2004). It can be argued that failing to detect population recovery or loss could carry greater conservation risks than treating a truly stable population as increasing or decreasing. For this reason we did not adjust our counts to reduce errors associated with false deviations from stability.[4]

In addition to breeding birds, we also examined existing data and literature findings on the status and trends for three species groups that are of broad conservation concern. These broad species groups included amphibians, bats, and pollinators. The widespread and rapid declines that have been observed among amphibians (Houlahan and others 2000; Mendelson and others 2006; Alford 2011; Wake 2012) are a generally recognized global phenomenon that prompted the completion of the first global amphibian assessment in 2004 (Stuart and others 2004). The previous RPA Assessment (*cf.* Flather and others 1999) had access to limited data on status and trends in amphibians—with much of the discussion focused on the work of Vial and Saylor (1993) and the summarization of the occurrence of amphibian populations that were determined to be of conservation concern across RPA regions. To provide some continuity with the previous Assessment and its synthesis of Vial and Saylor (1993), we re-examined the occurrence of at-risk amphibians (genera, species, and subspecies) by RPA region with data obtained from NatureServe (2010, 2011). We supplemented occurrence patterns of at-risk amphibians with actual species occupancy trend estimates based on the Amphibian Research and Monitoring Initiative (ARMI). This program was initiated in 2000 and was established as a network of independent research projects located among 39 monitoring areas across the United States. We review initial occupancy trend analyses from 118 time series ranging from 2 to 9 years over the 2002–2011 period for 50 species of amphibians as reported in Adams and others (2012).

Some species of bats have undergone equally rapid population declines stemming from the introduction of a non-native pathogen causing white-nose syndrome among species that hibernate in the United States (Gargas and others 2009; Frick and others 2010; Warnecke and others 2012). Although there have been broad-scale assessments of bat population status and trends (see Ellison and others 2003), recently observed population declines that have raised concern for regional extirpation among several bat species have occurred since publication of the 2000 RPA Assessment (*cf.* Flather and others 1999). We summarize the findings from published broad-scale assessments and review the geographic distribution of white-nose syndrome incidence over time and by county since its discovery using the monitoring data compiled and maintained by Bat Conservation International.[5]

The third species group of conservation concern is pollinators. There is a growing literature, both academic and in the wider media, documenting abundance and diversity declines among species that provide pollination services to flowering plants in both agricultural and natural ecosystems (Ghazoul 2005a; Potts and others 2010). We summarize the results from recent broad-scale assessments of pollinator status, including a recent review by the National

---

[4] Bird trend data are available from Michael S. Knowles (U.S. Forest Service, Rocky Mountain Research Station, Fort Collins, CO 80526, msknowles@fs.fed.us) and can be summarized according to individual user needs with respect to the multiple testing problem.

[5] http://www.batcon.org/index.php/what-we-do/white-nose-syndrome/

Research Council (2007) and Potts and others (2010). These reviews are further supplemented with data on avian pollinators from the BBS (http://www.mbr-pwrc.usgs.gov/bbs/bbs html) and data on the proportion of species that are of conservation concern based on NatureServe's conservation rankings.

Imperiled species

Given that ecosystem function is affected by the number and composition of species (Chapin and others 2000; Hector and others 2001; Loreau and others 2001; Cardinale and others 2006; Naeem and others 2012), then increases in species rarity—a trend that increases the prospect of extinction—would signal an erosion of the capacity of that system to deliver ecosystem services (Knapp 2011). Thus, a growing or diminishing list of species that are, by some set of criteria, considered imperiled has been used to indicate whether humans are conserving biological diversity and managing natural resources in a sustainable manner (Flather and Sieg 2000; USDA, Forest Service 2011) .

A number of classification systems have been developed for assigning species to categories of imperilment (for review see Flather and Sieg 2007). Perhaps the most familiar legislated system is defined by the Endangered Species Act of 1973 (ESA; P.L. 93-205, 87 Stat. 884, as amended). The ESA and its subsequent amendments codified broad-ranging protections for all species, plants or animals, and defines two categories of imperilment risk: (1) "endangered" refers to a species (subspecies or distinct population segment) that is in danger of extinction throughout all or a significant portion of its range (Sec. 3. [6]); and (2) "threatened" refers to a species that is likely to become an endangered species within the foreseeable future throughout all or a significant portion of its range (Sec. 3. [20]). Trends in the number of formally listed species by broad taxonomic groups were compiled from the Endangered Species Bulletin and the U.S. Fish and Wildlife Service's on-line box score that maintains the current count of U.S. threatened and endangered species (see Table 1).

Within the United States, one of the more comprehensively applied classification systems was developed by NatureServe and its network of natural heritage programs (Master 1991). This system is based on a number of criteria related to species occurrence, range size, population size, population trend, threats, fragility, and number of protected occurrences (Master and others 2000) that are used to assign species to nine conservation status ranks (Table 3). The use of NatureServe's rankings for comparison to the ESA listings was necessary to more fully examine species imperilment in light of findings suggesting that NatureServe's ranking criteria may be more objective than ESA listings because they are based purely on biological criteria while ESA listings are also affected by budget constraints, economic considerations as translated through the political process, judicial intervention, and variation in listing policy over time (Mehlman and others 2004; Laband and Neiswiadomy 2006; Brosi and Biber 2012). We also used NatureServe's data to document county-level occurrence of imperiled species using both ESA listings and NatureServe rankings. Geographic areas with concentrations of species listed as threatened or endangered were identified using the same procedure defined in the 2000 RPA Assessment (Flather and others 1999:56) to facilitate comparison. To account for the disparity in county area across the United States, counties were partitioned into "large-area" and "small-area" sets at a threshold of about 910,000 acres. Counties were then ranked

Table 3—Definition of conservation status ranks specified by NatureServe and its network of natural heritage programs (NatureServe 2010).

Rank	Definition
GX	**Presumed extinct** – Believed to be extinct throughout its range. Not located despite intensive searches of historical sites and other appropriate habitat, and virtually no likelihood of rediscovery.
GH	**Possibly extinct** – Known from only historical occurrences, but still may be extant; further searching needed.
G1	**Critically imperiled** – At very high risk of extinction due to extreme rarity or because of some factors making it especially vulnerable to extinction. Typically 5 or fewer occurrences or very few remaining individuals (<1,000) or acres (<2,000) or linear miles (<10).
G2	**Imperiled** – At high risk of extinction due to rarity or because of some factors making it very vulnerable to extinction. Typically 6 to 20 occurrences or few remaining individuals (1,000 to 3,000) or acres (2,000 to 10,000) or linear miles (10 to 50).
G3	**Vulnerable** – At moderate risk of extinction due to rarity, a restricted range (even if abundant at some locations), or because of other factors making it vulnerable to extinction. Typically 21 to 100 occurrences or between 3,000 and 10,000 individuals.
G4	**Apparently secure** – Uncommon but not rare (although it may be rare in parts of its range, particularly on the periphery) and usually widespread. Apparently not vulnerable in most of its range, but possibly cause for long-term concern. Typically more than 100 occurrences and more than 10,000 individuals.
G5	**Secure** – Common, widespread, and abundant (although it may be rare in parts of its range, particularly on the periphery). Not vulnerable in most of its range. Typically with considerably more than 1,000 occurrences and more than 10,000 individuals.
GU	**Unrankable** – Currently unrankable due to the lack of information or due to substantially conflicting information about status or trends.
GNR	**Not ranked** – Conservation status rank not yet assessed.

within these large- and small-area sets according to the number of threatened and endangered species that occurred within their boundaries. High concentrations of listed species were initially located by mapping the top 5 percent of large- and small-area counties (that is, those counties where the greatest number of listed species were found), following the criteria specified in Prendergast and others (1993).

Our purpose here is to review the trends and geographic patterns of imperiled species as an indicator of whether natural resources are being managed sustainably. In addition to examining listing trends and geographic patterns of occurrence among species formally listed under the ESA, we also looked at two classes of species using NatureServe conservation ranks (Table 3). We define species to be **at-risk** if they are critically imperiled (G1), imperiled (G2), or vulnerable (G3); and species to be of **conservation concern** if they are at-risk or are classified as one of the two categories of species that may already be extinct (presumed extinct [GX] or possibly extinct [GH]). Our findings will highlight, in particular, those changes that have occurred since the 2000 RPA Assessment as a way of judging whether the status of biodiversity is improving or becoming more impoverished.

Projecting Forest Bird Richness

As human populations grow, more and more of a landscape's native habitats are lost to agriculture, road construction, or urbanization. One of the more general signs that such land conversions may be stressing ecosystems is a reduction in the variety of organisms inhabiting a given place (Rapport and others 1985). We used the BBS to provide data on forest bird richness on those survey routes that occur in ecoregions supporting forest vegetation. Data on land use and cover came from the National Land Cover Data (NLCD), which were derived from Landsat satellite imagery at 30 m resolution for the coterminous United States (Vogelmann and others 2001). Housing data were obtained from the U.S. Census (U.S. Census Bureau 2001). A circular buffer with a radius equal to half the length of a BBS route (~12 miles) was placed on the route's center and used to define land use and housing characteristics in proximity to each survey route. Based on these data we (1) described the current pattern of forest bird richness across the coterminous United States and (2) fitted statistical models that related forest bird richness to land use and housing variables as described in Pidgeon and others (2007). Models were estimated for the richness of all forest birds breeding in the coterminous United States and for the richness of forest birds grouped according to broad life-history characteristics including neotropical migrants (forest birds that winter south of the U.S.–Mexico border), ground nesting (forest birds that build their nest on or near the ground), interior nesting (forest birds that prefer to nest away from the edge of forest habitats), and synanthopes (forest birds that tolerate and thrive in habitats associated with human settlement). We used Bailey's ecoregions (Bailey 1995) at the province level (hereafter ecoregions) to select those ecoregions that predominantly supported forest vegetation. Forest-wide models (all ecoregions that support forest vegetation) were estimated for each bird group (for details see Pidgeon and others 2007).

The fitted empirical models from Pidgeon and others (2007) were used to forecast the likely response among forest bird groups to projected changes in land use and housing. The land use projections were completed for three different future scenarios that varied in their basic assumptions concerning how socioeconomic and demographic factors were expected to change from 2010 to 2060 (Table 4). The purpose of scenarios in the 2010 RPA Assessment is to characterize common demographic, socioeconomic, and technological driving forces underlying changes in resource condition and to evaluate the sensitivity of resource trends (in this case forest bird communities) to a feasible future range of these driving forces. Detailed background concerning the 2010 RPA scenarios is described in USDA, Forest Service (2012b). Land use change models provided decadal acreage estimates for broad land use categories that included urban, cropland, forest, pasture, and range as defined by Wear (2011). Decadal housing projections were derived from the 2008 Woods and Pool county forecasts (http://www.woodsandpoole.com/) up to 2030 as described in Radeloff and others (2010). To pair housing growth estimates with land use projections in decades beyond 2030, we assumed that housing density remained unchanged in the decades beyond 2030.

Because of the spatially incongruent observation units between the forest bird models (~12 mile buffers around BBS routes) and the land use projection models (county, private land only), forest bird response forecasts were based on the mean values of the predictor variables and forest bird richness estimates as the initial conditions in the projections. We then aggregated the county-level land use projections from Wear (2011) and the housing

Table 4—Key characteristics of 2010 RPA Assessment scenarios (for details see USDA, Forest Service 2012b) . Numbers in parentheses indicate the factors of change over the projection period. For example, U.S. GDP increases by a factor of 3.3 times between 2006 and 2060 for scenario RPA A1B (see Table 1 in USDA, Forest Service 2012a).

| | RPA Scenarios | | |
Characteristic	A1B	A2	B2
General Global Description	Globalization, Economic Convergence	Regionalism, Less Trade	Slow Change, Localized Solutions
Global Real GDP Growth (2010-2060)	High (6.2X)	Low (3.2X)	Medium (3.5X)
Global Population Growth (2010-2060)	Medium (1.3X)	High (1.7X)	Medium (1.4X)
Global Expansion of Primary Biomass Energy Production	High	Medium	Medium
U.S. GDP Growth (2006-2060)	Medium (3.3X)	Low (2.6X)	Low (2.2X)
U.S. Population Growth (2006-2060)	Medium (1.5X)	High (1.7X)	Low (1.3X)

projections from Woods and Poole to the ecoregional level and developed an index of land use change over each decadal time step from 2010 to 2060. Those indexed land use and housing changes reflected the relative change in each time step from the initial condition. Because land use change estimates are only relevant to private land ownership, we assumed that federal lands remained constant with respect to the land use categories over the projection period. The indices of land use and housing change were then used to project the mean values of the predictor variables from Pidgeon and others (2007). Those projected predicator values were then applied to the estimated models from Pidgeon and others (2007) to project forest bird richness responses by species group and ecoregion.

Results and Discussion

Given the diversity of species that are resident or common migrants to the United States, and the variety of ecosystems supporting those species during all or part of their life histories, it seems almost self-evident that any review of status and trends in wildlife resources will vary among the species groups considered in this assessment. Each species group, and each species in those groups, will have varying habitat requirements and will be exposed to varying sets of environmental conditions owing to their unique footprint (that is, their geographic range) on the landscape. For these reasons, we see wide variation in species' responses to shifting environmental conditions, and we review those varied trends here.

Big and Small Game

Trends in big game populations have shown a general pattern of increase since the mid-1970s (Figure 2). Among those big game species that are widespread (occurring in many states),

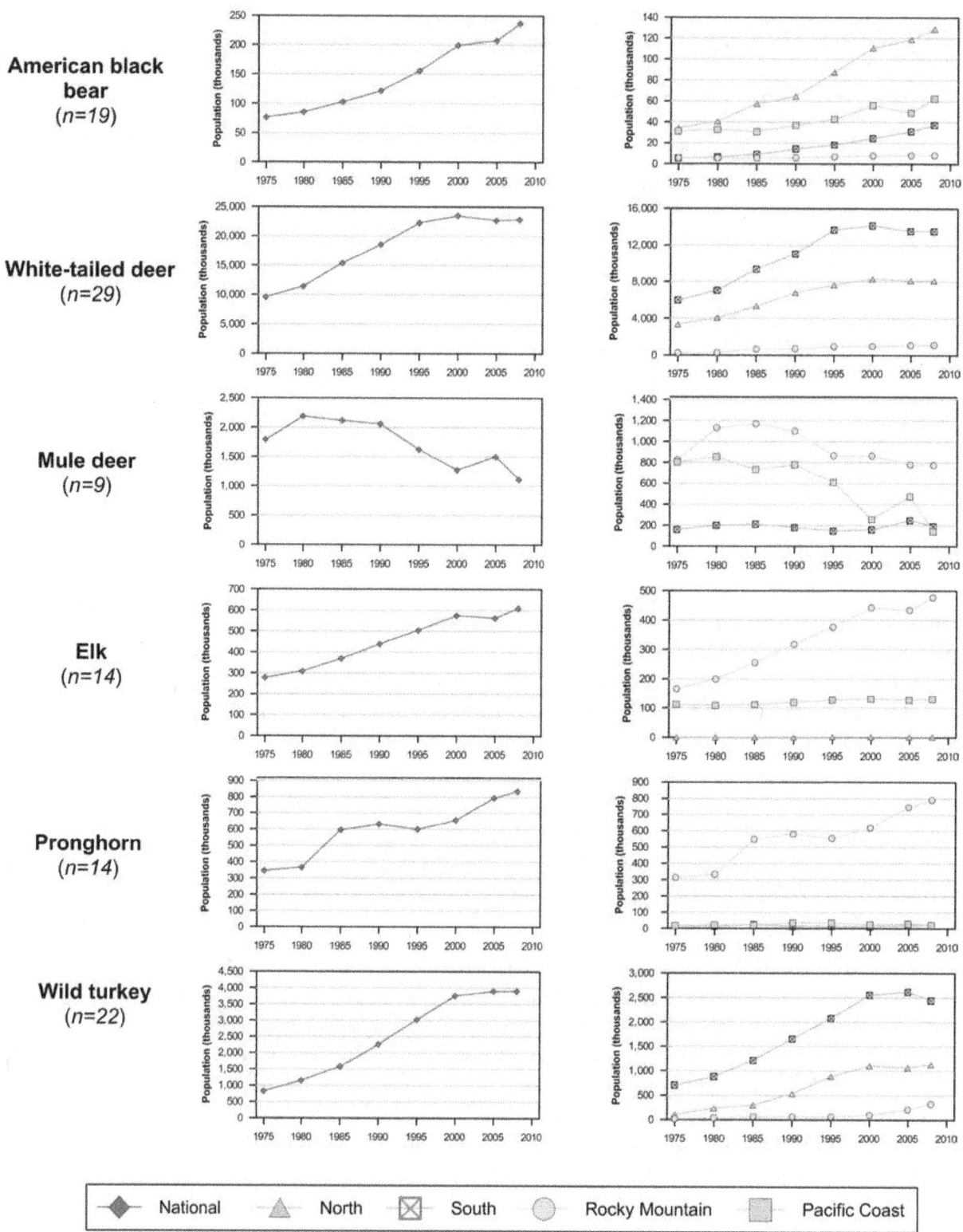

Figure 2—Population trends among selected widespread big game species for the nation and RPA regions from 1975 to 2008. The number of states providing population estimates is given by *n*, and regions lacking a trend line indicate that no state within that region (see Figure 1) provided population data for that particular species.

the most substantial increases nationally were observed among wild turkey, which grew at an annual rate of 4.8 percent. According to the BBS, wild turkey populations have grown in the long term (1966-2008) at an average annual rate of 8.8 percent. American black bear has also shown robust population growth at a 3.5 percent annual rate. White-tailed deer, pronghorn, and elk showed more modest but still strong positive annual growth at between 2.4 and 2.7 percent. Although white-tailed deer numbers continue to show increases in the long term, there is some evidence in the North and South regions that such population increases may not be sustainable. Since 2000, populations of white-tailed deer have remained relatively flat. Unlike population estimates of the other widespread big game species reviewed, mule deer population estimates have generally declined. Since 1980, mule deer populations have declined annually by 2.0 percent. The causes for the decline in mule deer are not well understood. Uncertainty in identifying definitive threats is attributable to a complex set of interacting factors, including weather, urban and residential development, oil and gas development, habitat loss and degradation, predation, and competitive interactions with other big game species (Unsworth and others 1999; Mule Deer Working Group 2004; Hurley and others 2011)—with the relative importance of each likely varying among different populations of this species. The recent and projected increases in oil and gas development in the Intermountain West (Copeland and others 2009) and noted mule deer avoidance of areas near well pads (Sawyer and others 2006) suggest that energy development on public lands may further erode the capacity of habitats to support mule deer.

Harvests generally follow population trends among widespread big game species (Figure 3). To examine if growth in harvests has matched growth in populations, we restricted our estimates of harvest growth to those states that also provided population estimates. Growth in harvest of wild turkey (4.8 percent) and elk harvests (2.4 percent) was nearly identical to population growth. Harvest growth among pronghorn has lagged behind population growth rates by nearly 2 percent. Because much of the habitat occupied by pronghorn occurs on private lands, or private landowners control access to pronghorn habitat on public lands, the failure of harvest to keep pace with population growth may be explained in part by inadequate hunter access to pronghorn (O'Gara and Morrison 2004). Harvest growth rates have also lagged behind population growth for black bear—a pattern that may be related to declining hunting participation (Mockrin and others 2012). Harvest growth rates among white-tailed and mule deer have actually exceeded population growth rates by about 1 percent. In the case of white-tailed deer, this may reflect intentional liberalization of the harvest in an attempt by state agencies to control what have become overabundant populations throughout much of their range (Côté and others 2004; Hurley and others 2012).

Small game populations are highly variable and some species show cyclical patterns. This variation can make it difficult to detect population trends. Moreover, few states were able to report small game population estimates in response to our data request. Among small game species groups, eight had sufficient population data from at least one state over the 1975-2008 period (Figure 4). However, the average number of states providing population estimates among these eight species groups was very small (fewer than two states). For this reason, our discussion of population trends based on state agency data is highly uncertain.

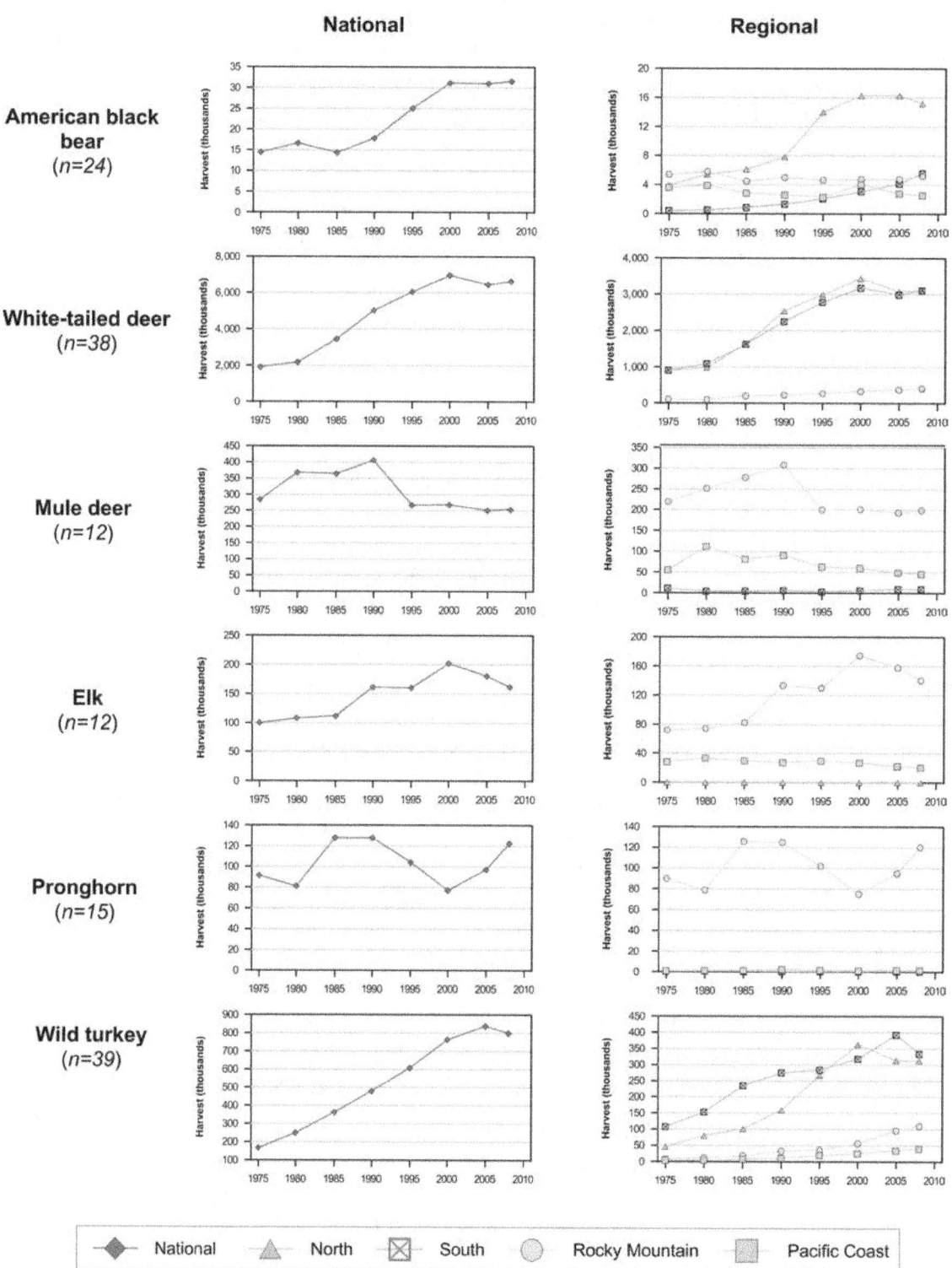

Figure 3—Harvest trends among selected widespread big game species for the nation and RPA regions from 1975 to 2008. The number of states providing harvest estimates is given by *n*, and regions lacking a trend line indicate that no state within that region (see Figure 1) provided harvest data for that particular species.

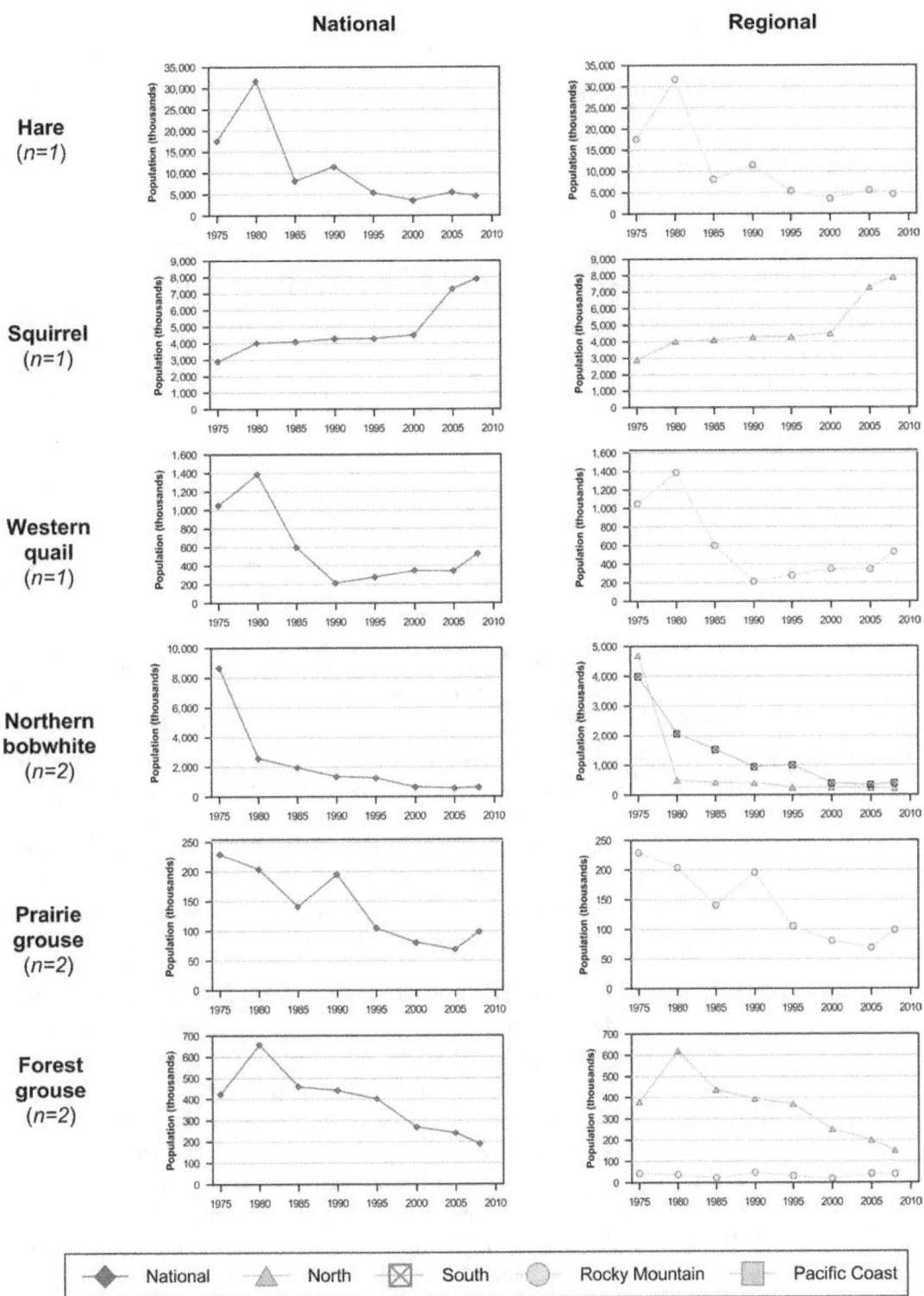

Figure 4—Population trends among selected small game species or species groups for the nation and RPA regions from 1975 to 2008. The number of states providing population estimates is given by *n,* and regions lacking a trend line indicate that no state within that region (see Figure 1) provided population data for that particular species or species group.

Figure 4—(Continued).

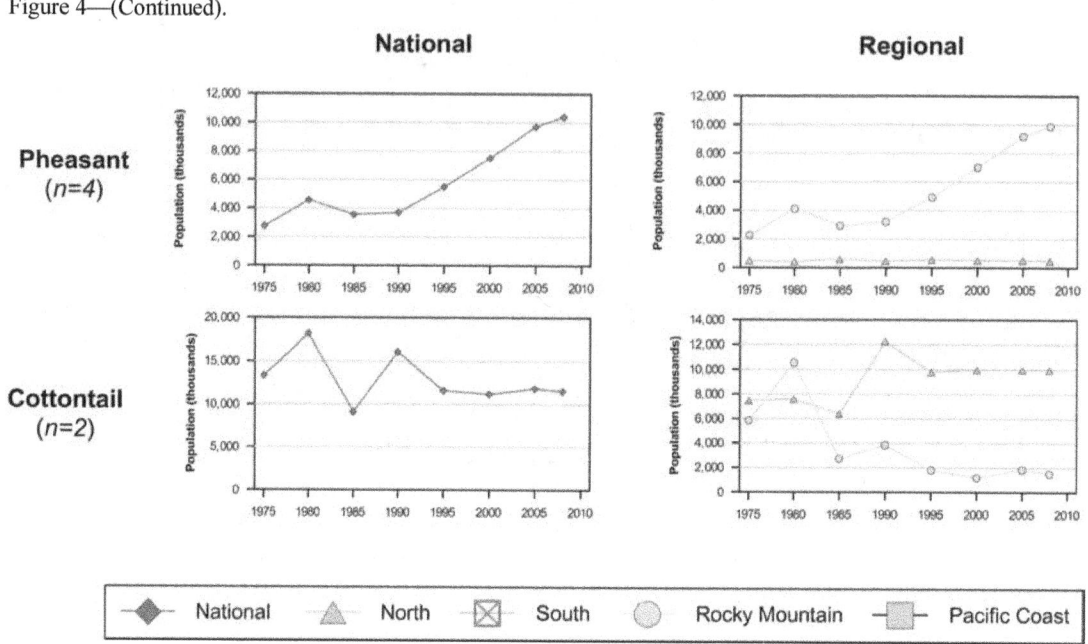

Of the eight small game species groups, five show evidence of decline over the 1975-2008 period: hare, western quail, northern bobwhite, prairie grouse, and forest grouse (Figure 4). Cottontail population estimates showed high variability prior to 1995, showing little evidence of a trend since then based on data from two states. Squirrel and ring-necked pheasant have shown evidence of long-term increases among the states providing estimates. Pheasant, with four states reporting population trends, increased at an annual pace of 4.1 percent over the 33-year period, with particularly strong increases since 1990. The national pattern is driven primarily by reported population increases in the Rocky Mountain region, and there is some geographically broad evidence that these gains may be attributed to the enrollment of agricultural lands into the Conservation Reserve Program (CRP, Nielson and others 2008).

Because so few states reported long-term trends in small game populations, a more representative picture of small game population trends, at least among upland game birds, required the use of the BBS (Figure 5). Most species showed little evidence of population increases or declines at the national or regional level. Of the 88 long-term (1966-2008) and short-term (1997-2008) population trend estimates depicted in Figure 5, more than half (57 percent) showed no statistical evidence of a trend. Northern bobwhite has shown the most substantial and geographically consistent population declines among all species. Annual population declines in the long term have averaged 3.8 percent and in the short term 4.2 percent— declines that have been attributed to urban development, intensive agriculture, and habitat fragmentation (Williams and others 2004). Scaled quail populations have also shown consistent patterns of decline, but not of the same magnitude as northern bobwhite—declining at an average annual rate of 2.0 percent and 2.7 percent in the long and short term, respectively. In addition to the factors implicated in bobwhite declines, scaled quail declines have also been

Species	Long Term 1966 2008					Short Term 1997 2008				
	National	North	South	Rocky Mountain	Pacific Coast	National	North	South	Rocky Mountain	Pacific Coast
Native										
Northern bobwhite	↘	↘	↘	↘	•	↘	↘	↘	↘	•
Mountain quail	−	•	•	•	−	−	•	•	•	−
Scaled quail	↘	•	↘	−	•	↘	•	−	↘	•
California quail	↗	•	•	↗	↗	↗	•	•	+	↗
Gambel s quail	+	•	•	+	+	+	•	•	+	+
Blue grouse	+	•	•	↗	−	↗	•	•	↗	+
Ruffed grouse	+	−	−	+	−	+	+	−	+	+
Greater prairie chicken	+	+	•	↗	•	↗	+	•	↗	•
Sharp tailed grouse	+	↗	•	+	•	+	↗	•	+	•
Sage grouse	↘	•	•	↘	−	−	•	•	−	+
Non native										
Gray partridge	−	+	•	−	↘	+	+	•	−	−
Chukar	+	•	•	+	−	+	•	•	↗	−
Ring necked pheasant	−	↘	↗	+	↘	↗	↘	↗	↗	↘

Figure 5—Long-term (1966–2008) and short-term (1997–2008) population trends in upland game birds for the Nation and RPA regions from the North American Breeding Bird Survey. Bolded arrows and color (blue=increasing; red=decreasing) indicate the direction of significant ($P<0.05$) trends; red minus (−) and blue plus (+) indicate the direction of a trend that was not determined to be significantly different from stable ($P\geq0.05$). Missing value entries (•) indicate there was an insufficient number of routes (<15) to estimate a trend.

associated with grazing, brush control, and conversion of diverse native grasslands to monocultures of exotic grasses to increase forage for cattle production (Brennan and others 2005). Long-term declines are also evident with sage grouse nationally (-4.2 percent per year) and within the Rocky Mountains (-4.3 percent per year)—declines that have been attributed to habitat degradation in the longer term (Knick and others 2003) and to energy development, invasion of non-native plant species, and disease (West Nile virus) in the near term (Aldridge and others 2008; Naugle and others 2011). California quail is the only species of upland game bird that showed evidence of both long-term (+1.0 percent per year) and short-term (+2.4 percent per year) population increases at the national level. Short-term population increases were observed for blue grouse (+3.1 percent per year) and greater prairie-chicken (+12.8 percent per year). Ring-necked pheasant has shown mixed population trends, with long-term declines in the North (-2.0 percent per year) and Pacific Coast (-2.3 percent year), but increases in the South (+2.1 percent per year). In the short term, ring-necked pheasant continued its decline in the North and Pacific Coast regions, but those declines were more than offset by population increases in the South and Rocky Mountain regions such that a modest increase (+1.6 percent per year) was detected at the national level.

The general pattern of small game harvests (Figure 6) is one of declining trends at both the national and regional levels. The substantial decline in the number of hunters pursuing small game (Mockrin and others 2012) has undoubtedly played a role in these harvest declines. Northern bobwhite harvests have dropped by more than 15 million birds from 1975 to 2008 among reporting states. Such a decline translated into an average annual loss of 5.7 percent— a rate of decline largely driven by what has occurred in the North and South RPA regions. Cottontail harvests have declined by an even greater magnitude (24 million animals) with annual reductions since 1975 averaging 4.5 percent. Although the magnitude of harvest decline among hares was much more modest (nearly 2 million animals), that decline translated into the greatest average annual decline of 7.2 percent per year. More modest declines were observed for western quail (-3.9 percent per year), squirrel (-2.9 percent per year), forest grouse (-2.9 percent per year), and prairie grouse (-2.6 percent per year). The only species deviating from this pattern of broad harvest decline was pheasant in the South and Rocky Mountain regions, where harvests estimates indicated a general increase in the number of birds bagged since the mid-1980s.

Migratory Game Birds

Nearly half of the native landbirds occurring in North America depend on habitats occurring in at least two of the three largest countries (Canada, United States, and Mexico) making up the continent, and nearly 40 percent of these species traverse the continent twice a year (Berlanga and others 2010:5, 18). A much smaller percentage of these species are actually regulated as harvested game species in the United States. Because of the distances traveled by these species over the course of their annual cycle, international agreements and cooperation have played a significant role in their conservation and management. Here we review the population and harvest trends among those native migratory game bird species that are commonly sought by hunters including the nearly 50 species of waterfowl (ducks, geese, and swans) (Sibley 2000) and two migratory upland game bird species (mourning dove and woodcock).

Waterfowl

Breeding **duck** population estimates in 2010 were 21 percent higher than the long-term (1955-2009) average, and duck populations have shown a general increasing trend since the early 2000s (Figure 7). After reaching a record low in 1990 (25.1 million birds), the total duck population increased nearly 63 percent to 40.9 million birds by 2010. Since the 2000 RPA Assessment, duck populations peaked at nearly 44 million birds in the late 1990s only to drop below 32 million birds during the drought years of the early- to mid-2000s (Figure 7). Although breeding populations have been generally favorable since the mid-2000s (exceeding 40 million birds in three of the five years from 2006 to 2010), it is important to note that the overall target breeding population for ducks is 62 million birds as specified in the North American Waterfowl Plan (USDI, Fish and Wildlife Service and others 1994). Furthermore, there is concern that population gains observed since 2005 may be jeopardized by recent Supreme Court rulings that remove isolated wetlands, like those characterizing the prairie pothole region, from federal regulation, potentially exposing those wetlands to conversion or degradation (Leibowitz 2003; Tiner 2003; Zinn and Copeland 2006).

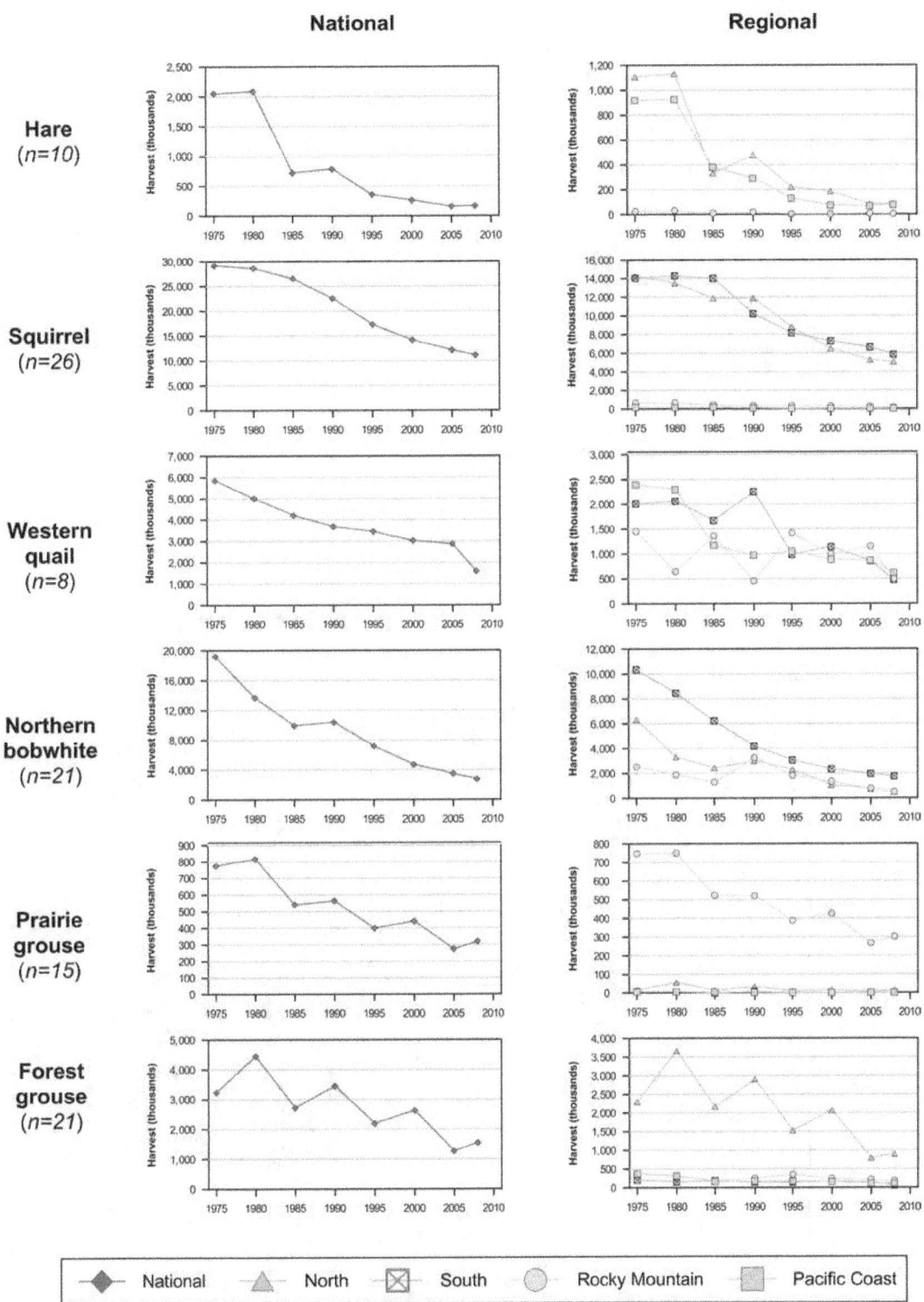

Figure 6—Harvest trends among selected small game species or species groups for the nation and RPA regions from 1975 to 2008. The number of states providing harvest estimates is given by *n*, and regions lacking a trend line indicate that no state within that region (see Figure 1) provided harvest data for that particular species or species group.

Figure 6—(Continued).

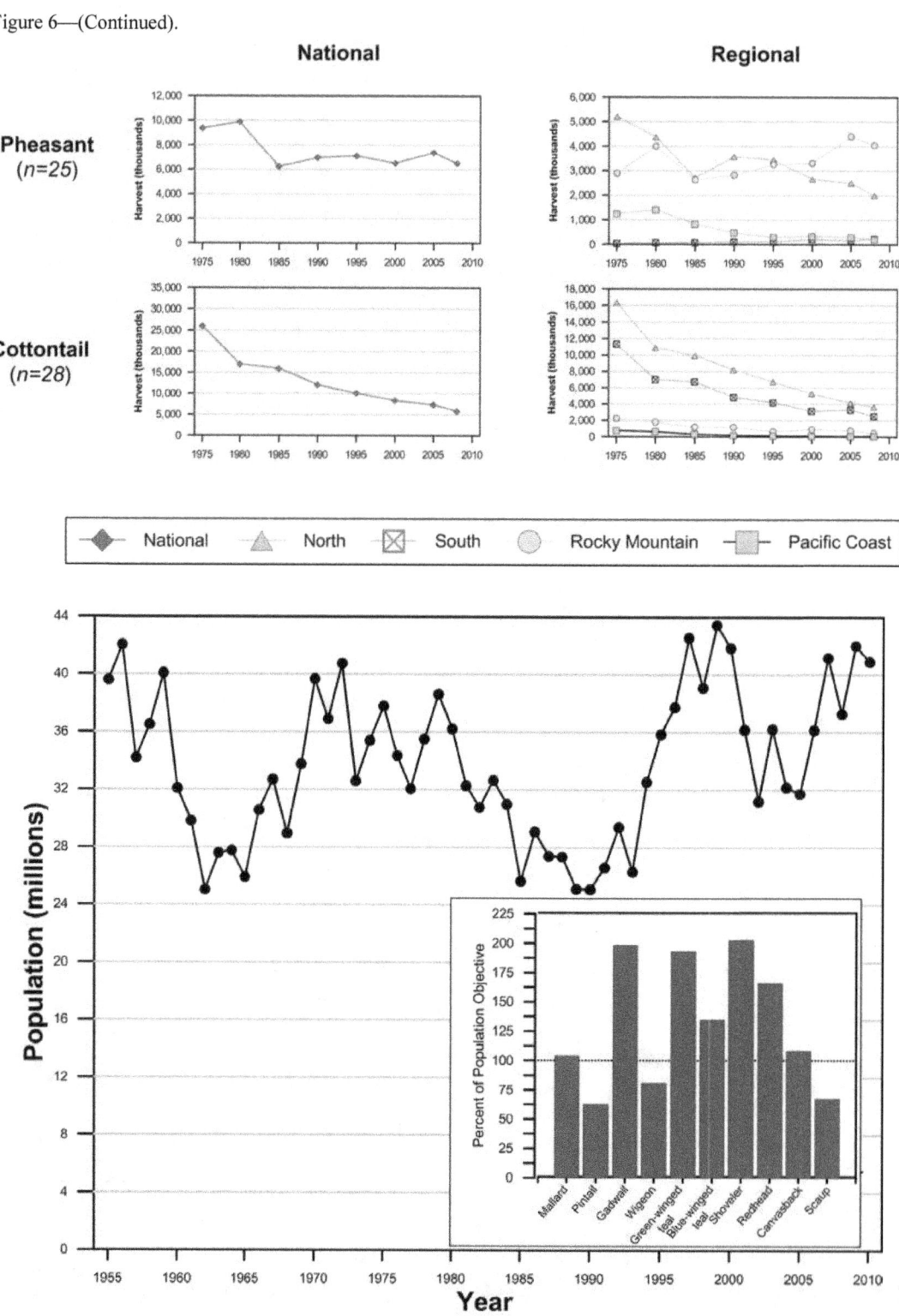

Figure 7—Trend in the duck population from 1955 to 2010 and the relation between 2010 population estimates for the 10 principal duck species (inset) and population objectives specified in the North American Waterfowl Plan measured as percent of objective (USDI, Fish and Wildlife Service and others 1994).

Breeding population trends among the 10 most common duck species have been variable. Seven of the ten most common species have 2010 breeding populations that exceed their long-term means with green-winged teal, shoveler, gadwall, and redhead exceeding those averages by more than 60 percent. The 2010 breeding population of the most abundant duck, mallard (8.4 million), exceeds its long-term average by 12 percent. Of the seven species exceeding their long-term means, five have shown evidence of benefiting from CRP enrollments in the Prairie Pothole region of the northern plains (Reynolds and others 2001; Haufler 2005). Three duck species remain below their long-term average breeding populations: scaup (-16 percent), northern pintail (-13 percent), and American widgeon (-7 percent). These same three species also remained below the population objectives specified in the North American Waterfowl Plan (Figure 7[inset]). These three species were also highlighted in the 2000 RPA Assessment as species of management concern. Identification of the factors responsible for the persistent management concerns among these three species remains uncertain. However, research directed at understanding these dynamics implicate agricultural intensification in key pintail breeding areas (Podruzny and others 2002), degradation of wetland habitats used by pintails during migration and for wintering causing a decline in body condition (Moon and others 2007), and contamination and lower female survivorship among scaup (Afton and Anderson 2001).

Given that harvests of ducks are established adaptively with population monitoring data feeding the decision process for setting harvest regulations (Nichols and others 2007), it is not surprising that harvest trends mirror breeding population trends (Figure 8). After a near tripling of the duck harvest during the 1960s, national harvests hovered around 13.5 million birds during the 1970s. Harvests declined dramatically during the 1980s, reaching a low of 4.7 million birds in 1988, in response to troubling population declines. Since then, harvests rebounded substantially, reaching a peak of 17 million birds in the late 1990s. Harvests have recently fluctuated around 13 million birds—levels that were observed during the 1970s.

Because waterfowl have long been managed according to flyways—the four major routes taken by migrating birds—we present regional trends in harvest according to those administrative units that include the Atlantic, Mississippi, Central, and Pacific flyways. Since the 2000 RPA Assessment (from 1995 onward), the Mississippi flyway has accounted for about 47 percent of the harvest (Figure 8). Harvests in the Pacific and Central flyways have been evenly split at around 20 percent. Harvests in the Atlantic flyway have been, relatively speaking, more stable—around 1.7 million birds or 12 percent of the national harvest. All flyways tend to show the same qualitative pattern of declining harvests during the 1980s—substantial gains during the 1990s and early-2000s, followed by a retraction to harvest levels observed during the 1970s.

Populations of **geese and swans** (including Canada goose, brant, snow goose, Ross's goose, emperor goose, white-fronted goose, and tundra swan) are monitored by surveying 30 separate population segments. A total of 11 populations showed at least marginal evidence ($P<0.15$) of increases over the 2001 to 2010 period, and 16 populations showed no evidence of a trend. Therefore, 90 percent of goose and swan populations were determined to be stable or increasing since 2000—an increase of 10 percent over the 2000 RPA Assessment. Two populations (Atlantic Flyway resident population of Canada geese and dusky Canada geese) showed at least marginal evidence ($P<0.15$) of population declines since 2001 (Figure 9a, d).

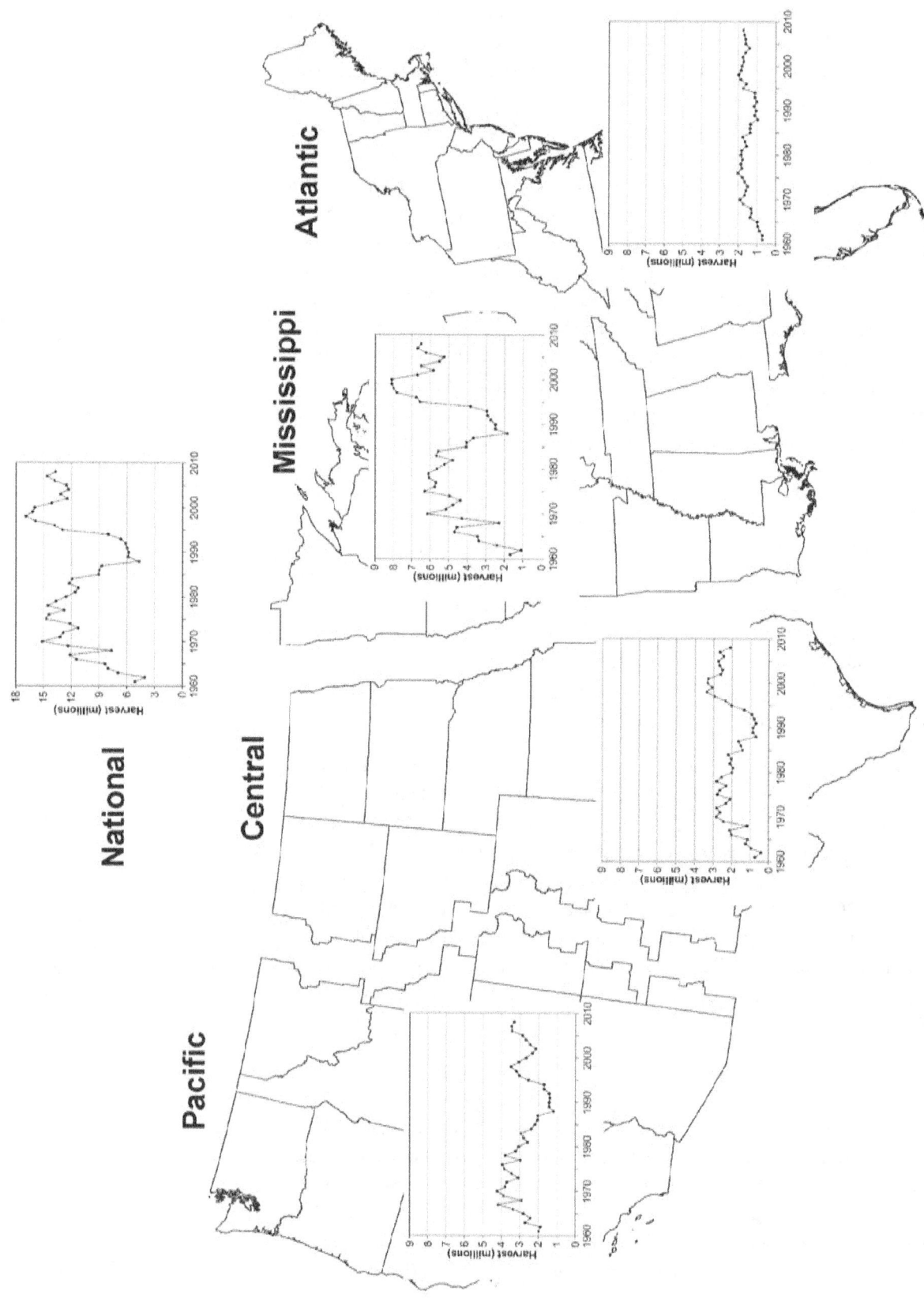

Figure 8—Trends in total duck harvests from 1961 to 2008 for the nation and by administrative flyway.

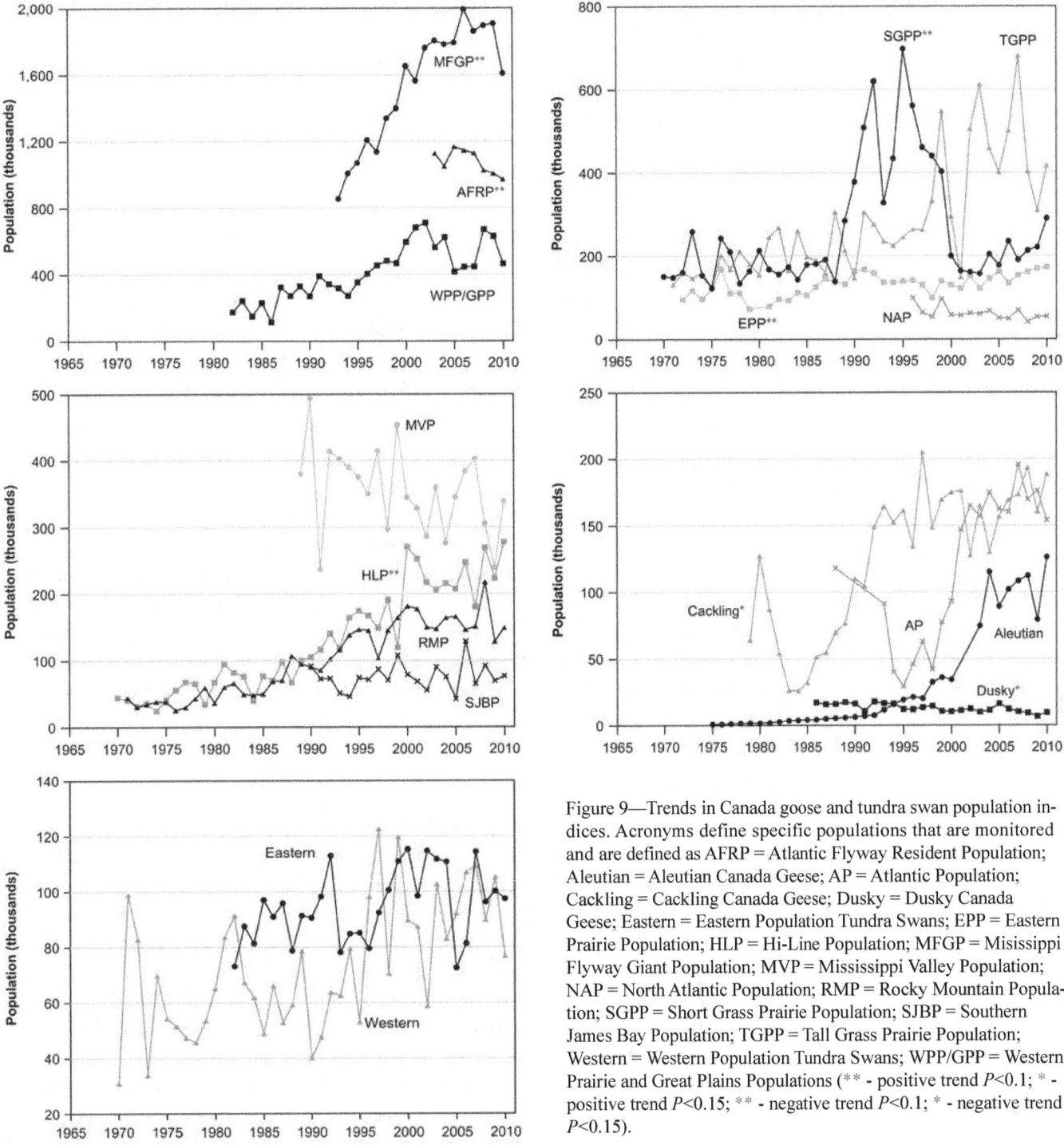

Figure 9—Trends in Canada goose and tundra swan population indices. Acronyms define specific populations that are monitored and are defined as AFRP = Atlantic Flyway Resident Population; Aleutian = Aleutian Canada Geese; AP = Atlantic Population; Cackling = Cackling Canada Geese; Dusky = Dusky Canada Geese; Eastern = Eastern Population Tundra Swans; EPP = Eastern Prairie Population; HLP = Hi-Line Population; MFGP = Misissippi Flyway Giant Population; MVP = Mississippi Valley Population; NAP = North Atlantic Population; RMP = Rocky Mountain Population; SGPP = Short Grass Prairie Population; SJBP = Southern James Bay Population; TGPP = Tall Grass Prairie Population; Western = Western Population Tundra Swans; WPP/GPP = Western Prairie and Great Plains Populations (** - positive trend *P*<0.1; * - positive trend *P*<0.15; ** - negative trend *P*<0.1; * - negative trend *P*<0.15).

All other population segments of Canada geese have increasing or stable trends with statistically notable (P<0.1) increases since 2001 being observed among the eastern prairie, Mississippi Flyway giant, short grass prairie, and hi-line populations (Figure 9). Some of the greatest population gains during the 2000s have been observed among species collectively referred to as "light geese"—referring to both snow geese and Ross's geese. Since 2001, three out of the five monitored populations have shown average annual population increases that equal or exceed 5 percent. The greatest population gains among all geese have been observed in the Western Central Flyway population of light geese, which has increased an average of 11 percent per year since 2001. Such population gains among light geese have been a management concern since the mid-1990s because, by many criteria, these species qualify as overabundant (Alisauskas and others 2011), with documented habitat degradation on both the breeding and wintering grounds (Ankney 1996). Population trends among tundra swan populations (Figure 9e) are highly variable and neither the western (2 percent increase per year since 2001) nor the eastern populations (1 percent decrease per year since 2001) show a statistically detectable trend over the last decade.

The general increasing trend in goose populations is reflected in goose harvest trends. Since the early 1990s there has been a steady and substantial increase in the goose harvests nationally and across all flyways (Figure 10). The one region showing a deviation from this pattern is the Central Flyway—after reaching a peak harvest in 2000, the number of geese taken by hunters has declined by nearly 34 percent. Although it has been suggested that hunting could be used to address the overabundance of light geese (Menu and others 2002), liberalization of harvest regulations under a conservation order aimed at reducing population growth of mid-continent light geese failed to reduce the number of breeding adults, suggesting that goose numbers exceed the ability of waterfowl hunters (see Mockrin and others 2012) to impose sufficient mortality to shift the current population trajectory (Alisauskas and others 2011). Swan harvest estimates, like their populations, have been variable, with little evidence of a trend (Figure 11).

Webless migratory

Both woodcock and mourning dove populations are monitored using call-count surveys that provide an annual index of abundance. **Woodcock** populations continue to show a long-term pattern of population decline (Figure 12) at an annual rate of nearly -1 percent over the 1968 to 2010 period. Over this period the call-count index has declined by more than 30 percent. Regional population trends in the Eastern and Central management areas do not deviate in any substantive way from the national singing-ground counts, suggesting that the causes for the declines are widespread. These trends in call-count indices are qualitatively consistent with North American Breeding Bird Survey trends— the latter showing an average annual decline for woodcock of 2.5 percent from 1966 to 2008 (J.R. Sauer, personal communication, U.S. Geological Survey, Biological Resources Division, Patuxent Wildlife Research Center, 2010). Recent harvest estimates for woodcock have also declined by more than 50 percent since 1999 in both management regions (Figure 13)—a pattern that likely reflects both woodcock population declines and a reduced numbers of hunters (see Mockrin and others 2012). Woodcock select early successional stages of second-growth hardwood forests associated with fields and forest openings on mesic sites (Keppie and Whiting 1994), and the widespread population declines noted in this species are due to declines in young forests in the east, land use intensification associated with agricultural production, and urbanization (Dessecker and McAuley 2001).

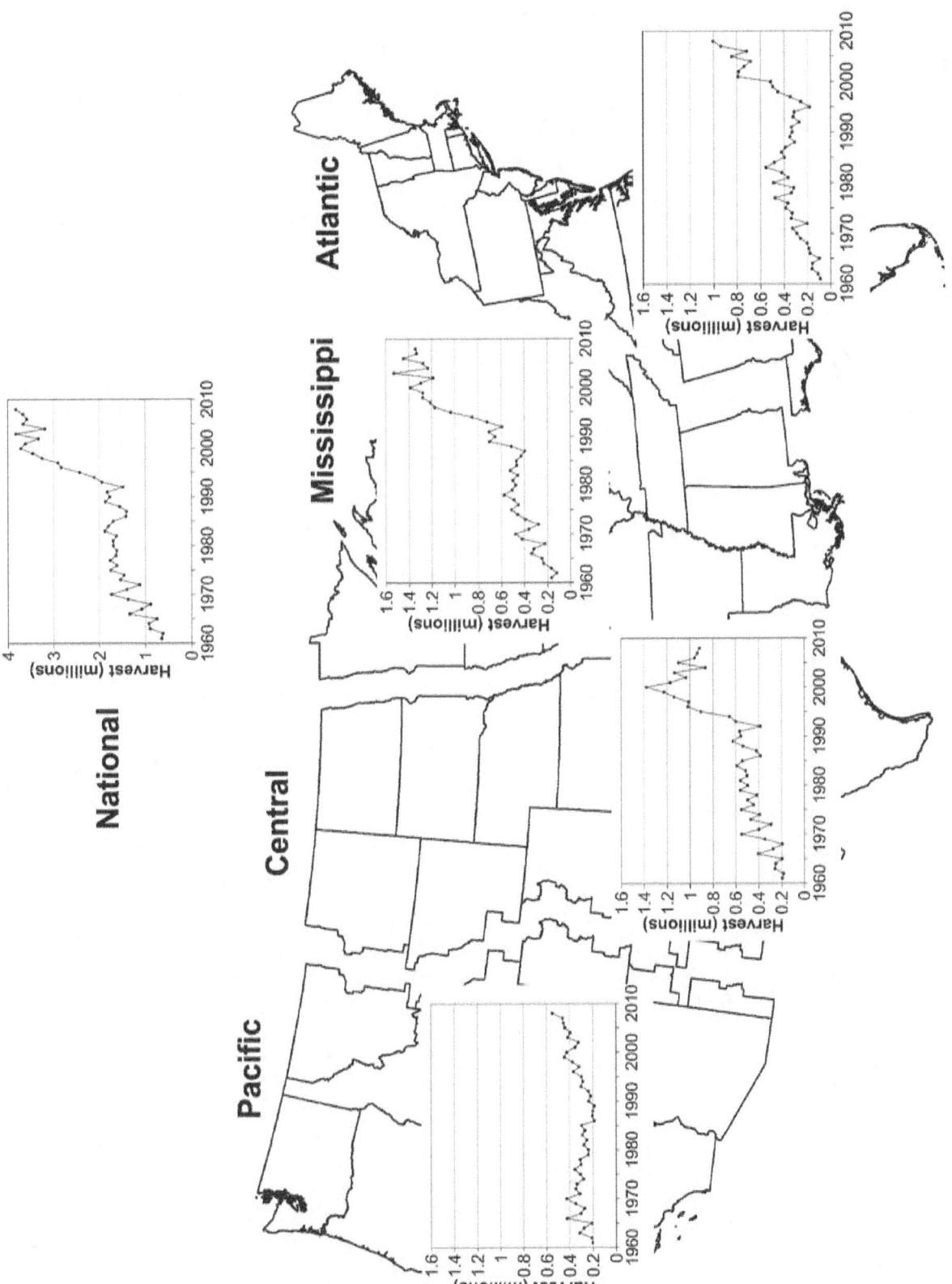

Figure 10—Trends in total goose harvests from 1961 to 2008 for the nation and by administrative flyway.

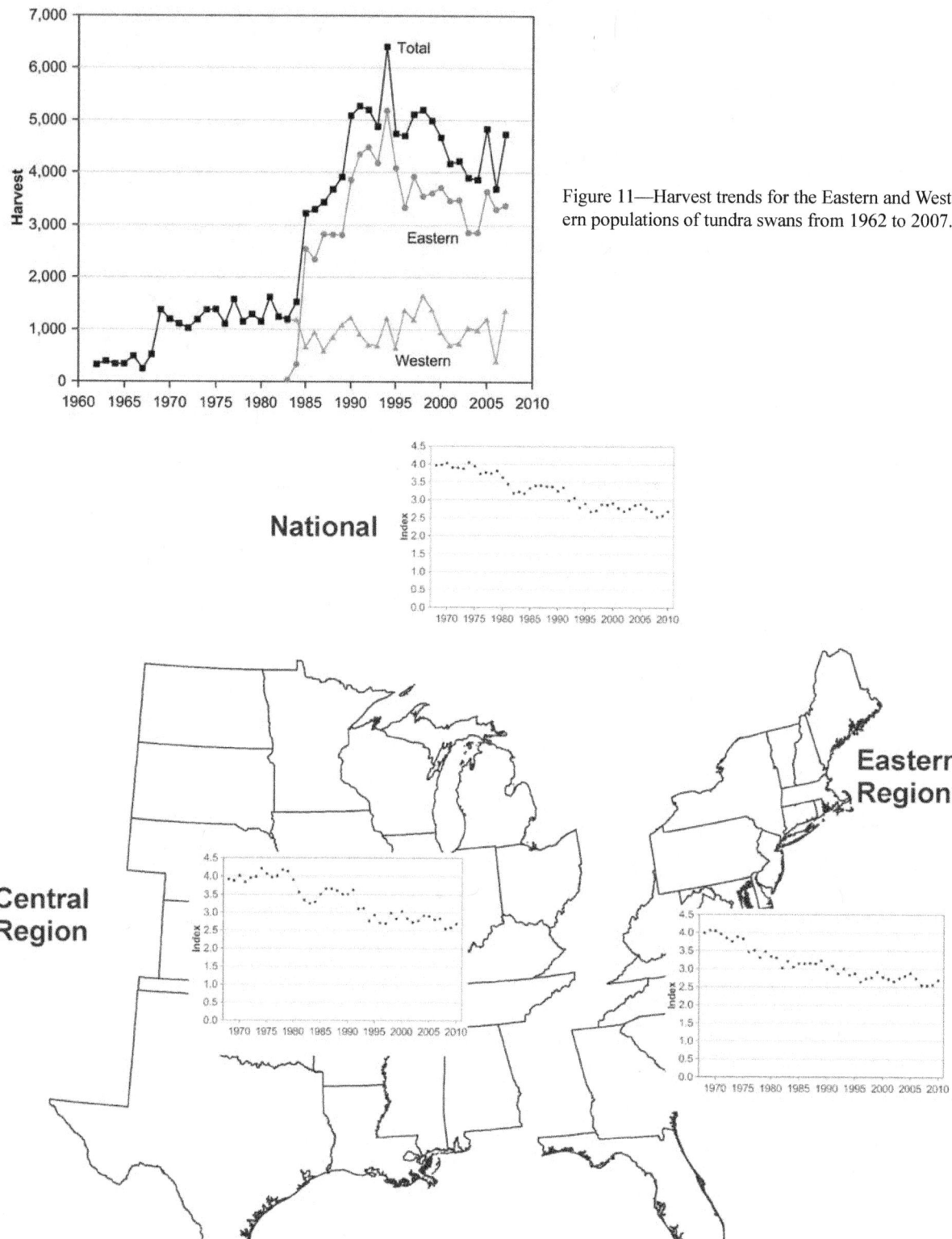

Figure 11—Harvest trends for the Eastern and Western populations of tundra swans from 1962 to 2007.

Figure 12—Woodcock population trends from 1968 to 2010 for the nation and by management region.

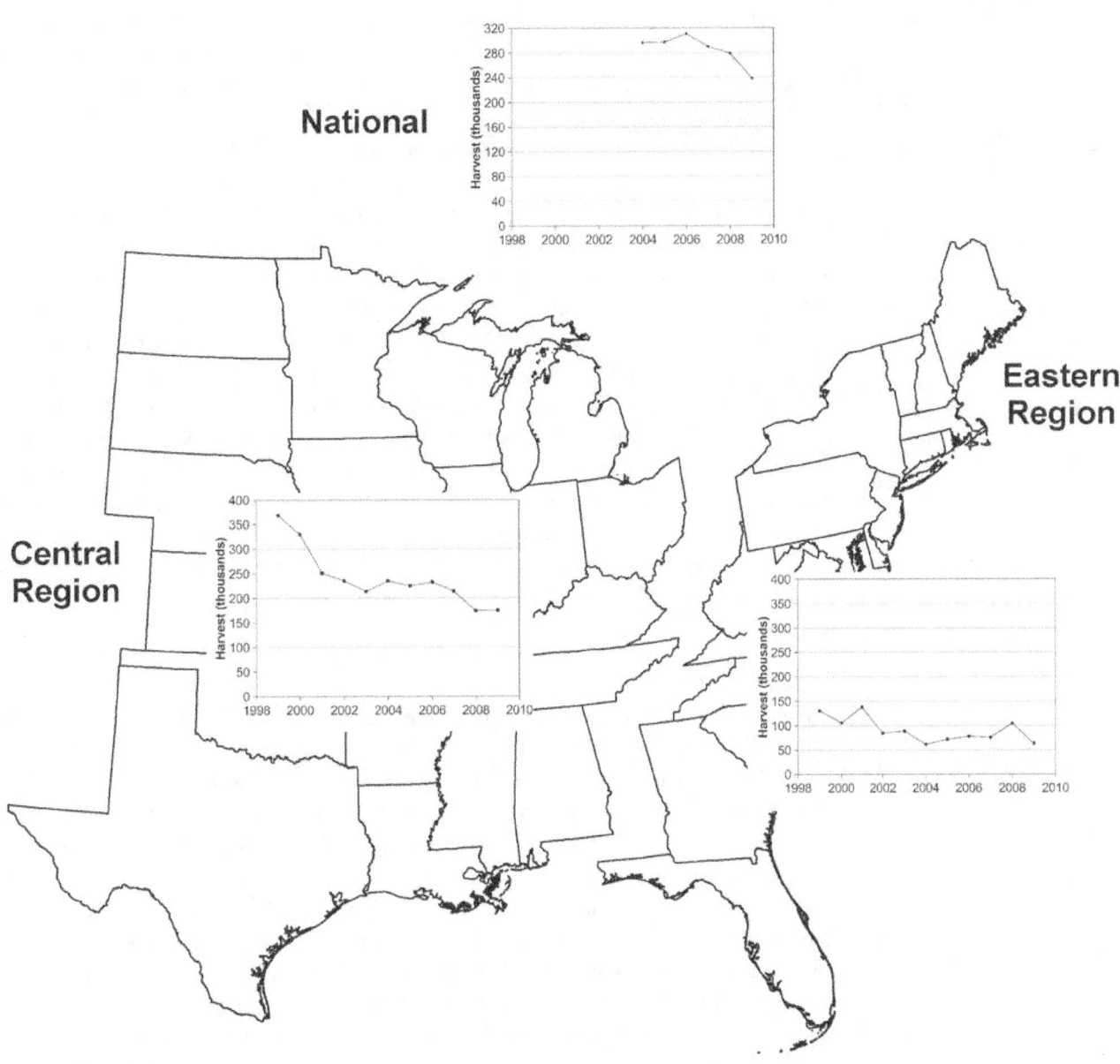

Figure 13—Woodcock harvest trends from 1999 to 2009 for the nation and by management region.

Although the birds are adapted to urban and rural landscapes, **mourning dove** abundance has declined across all three management regions since the mid-1960s. Unlike call count indices for woodcock, regional call-count indices for mourning dove indicate variable population declines with the greatest decline occurring in the Western management unit (-1.3 percent per year) and the smallest decline in the Eastern management unit (-0.3 percent per year). Cumulative declines in call indices were 45 percent, 22 percent, and 12 percent for the Western, Central, and Eastern management units, respectively (Figure 14). Again, population trends based on call-count indices are consistent with North American Breeding Bird Survey trends—the latter showing an average annual decline of 0.4 percent from 1966 to 2008 (J.R. Sauer, personal communication, U.S. Geological Survey, Biological Resources Division, Patuxent Wildlife Research Center, 2010). Like declines in woodcock, declines in mourning doves are thought to be caused by intensification of some agricultural practices such as expansion of improved pastureland, loss of shelter belts and fencerows, or removal of isolated forest patches (Reeves and others 1993; Tomlison and Dunks 1993). Furthermore, extensive plantings of pine monocultures in the South have been found to be detrimental to mourning dove populations (Mirarchi 2001). Harvests of doves have declined since 1999, with the greatest drop occurring in the Central management unit (-34 percent). Harvests in the Western management unit have actually increased slightly (+5.6 percent) since 1999 (Figure 15) despite the population declines indicated by call-count indices.

Furbearers

National trends in furbearer harvests show three distinct periods: a period of rapidly increasing harvests during the 1970s; a period of rapidly declining harvest during the 1980s; and a relatively stable harvest level since 1990 (Figure 16). After reaching a peak of 20 million pelts in 1979, harvests declined to 2.7 million pelts in 1990. Since the 2000 RPA Assessment (*cf.* Flather and others 1999), fur harvests have averaged approximately 4.4 million pelts per year. This represents a 61 percent drop in harvest from the average annual harvest observed during the period reported in the last Assessment (11.4 million pelts per year from 1970 to 1995). The 2000 RPA Assessment documented the strong influence of pelt prices on harvest (Flather and others 1999) with peak prices during the late 1970s and mid-1980s associated with peaks in harvest. Prices during the 1990s were about 60 percent below peak levels. The trend in fur harvest among the two most commonly harvested species (muskrat and raccoon) mirror the trends observed across all furbearer species (28 species) contributing to the national total (Figure 16).

There are notable geographic disparities in the fur harvest among RPA regions. The North has long dominated fur harvests, and since the 2000 RPA Assessment nearly 70 percent of all pelts came from the North (Figure 17). There has been a shift in regional contribution between the South and Rocky Mountain regions. In the last Assessment, the South contributed just over one quarter of all pelts to the total national harvest. Since then, the South's contribution has declined to around 11 percent, with the gap being made up primarily by gains in the Rocky Mountain region. Fur harvests in the Pacific Coast region have always contributed the least to the national total. Since 1995, the Pacific Coast states accounted for about 1 percent of total national harvest.

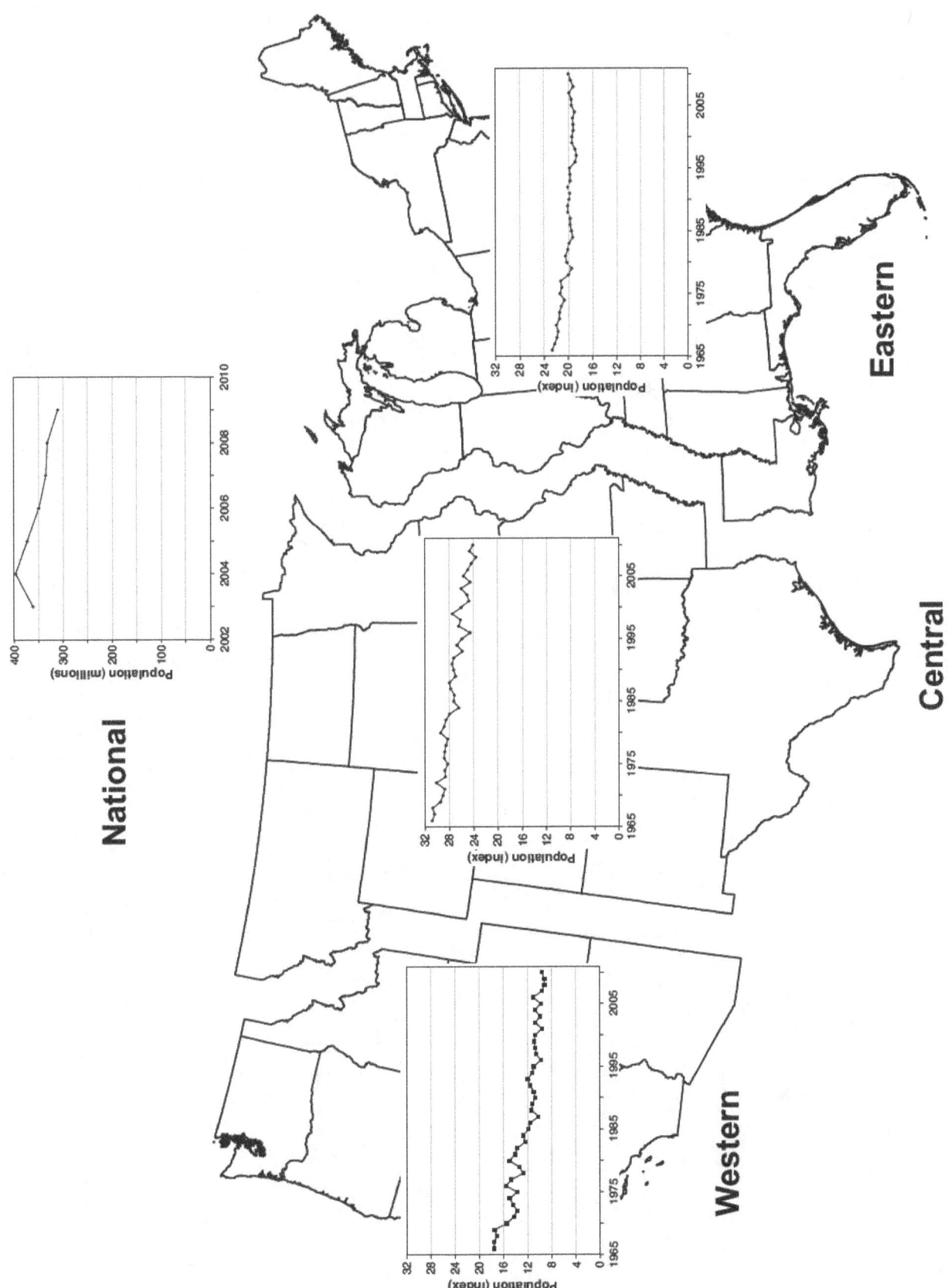

Figure 14—Mourning dove population trends from 1966 to 2010 for the nation and by management unit.

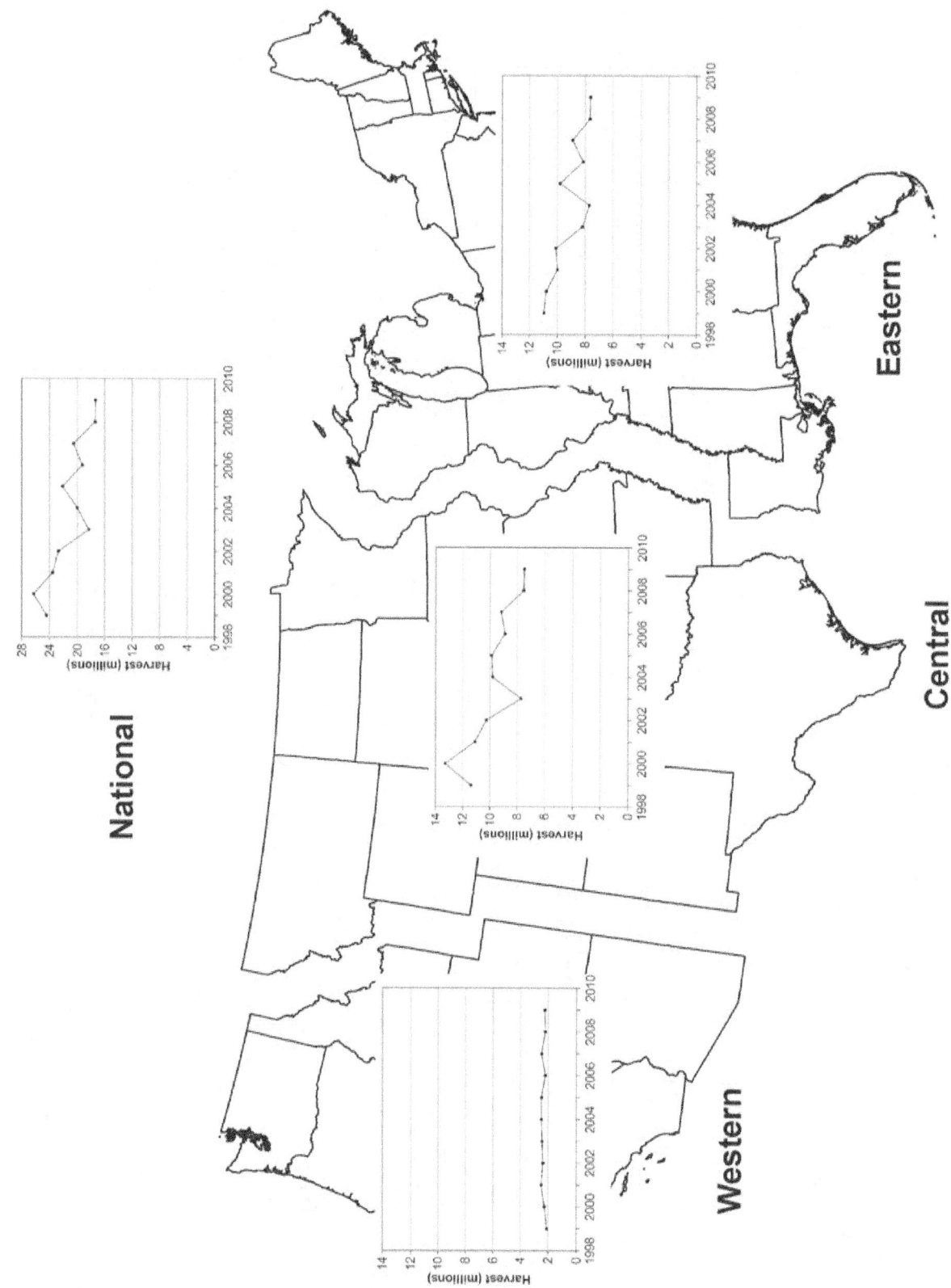

Figure 15—Mourning dove harvest trends from 1999 to 2009 for the nation and by management unit.

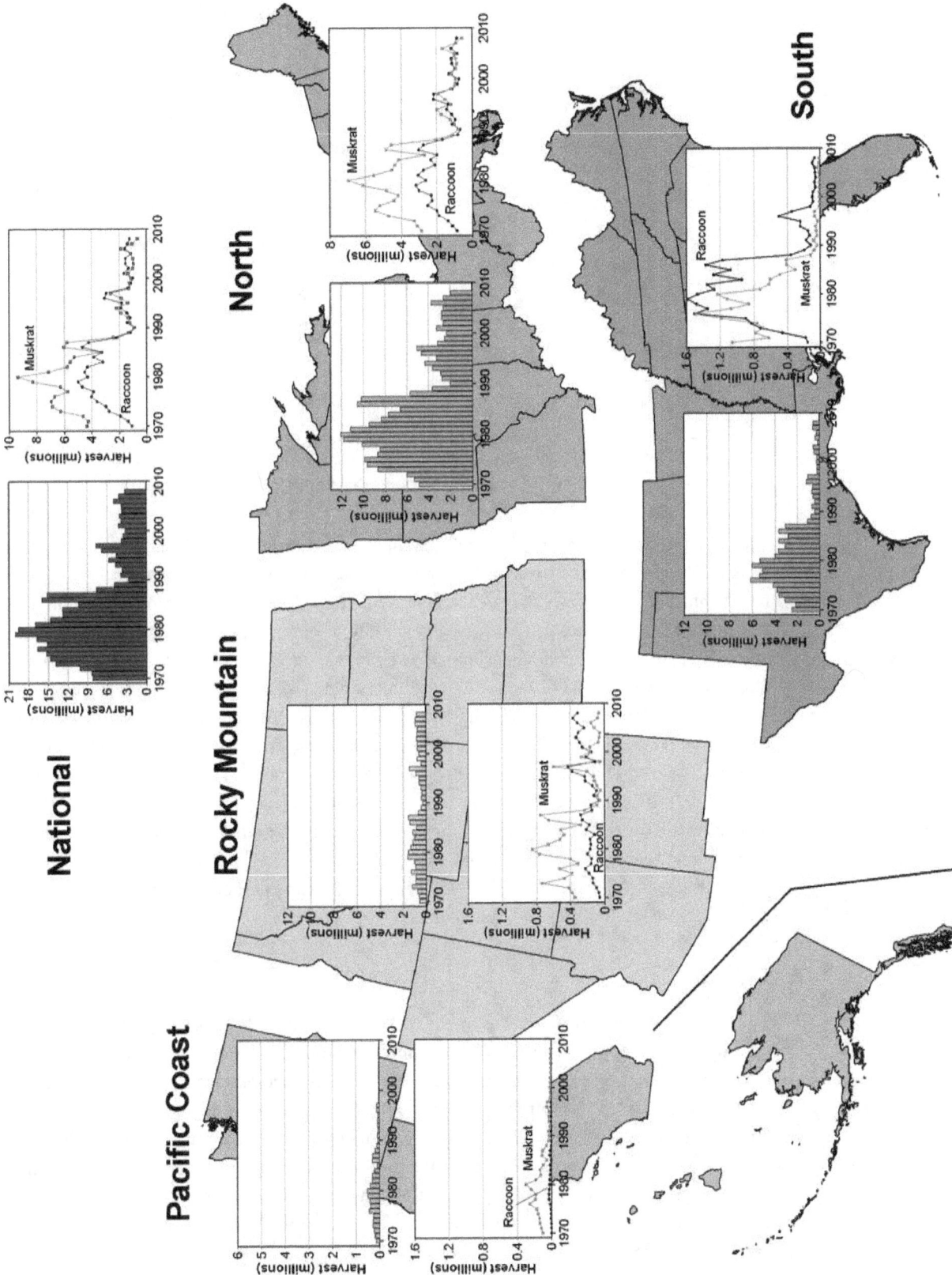

Figure 16—Trends in total fur harvest (bar graphs) and harvest of muskrat and raccoon (line graphs) for the nation and by RPA region from 1970 to 2008 (source: B. White, personal communication, Association of Fish and Wildlife Agencies and Missouri Department of Conservation, 2010).

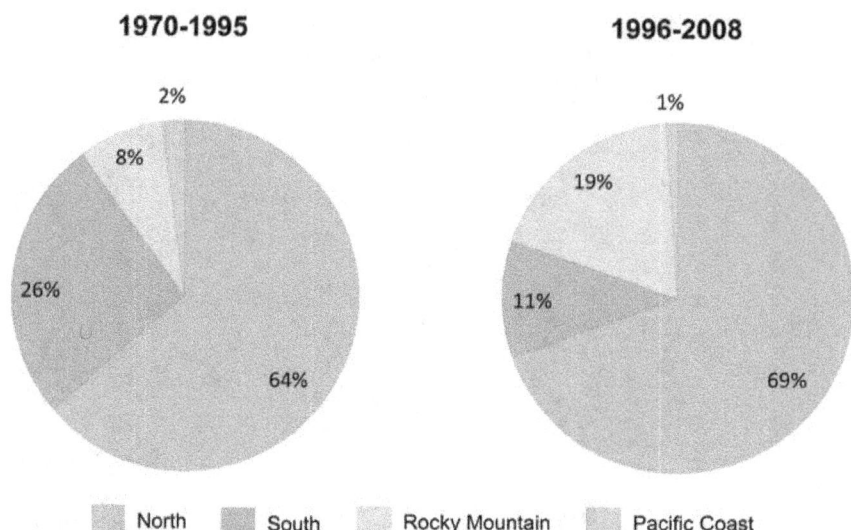

1970-1995   **1996-2008**

North   South   Rocky Mountain   Pacific Coast

Figure 17—Average relative (percent) fur harvest by RPA region for the 1970-1995 (2000 RPA Assessment) and 1996-2008 periods (source: B. White, personal communication, Association of Fish and Wildlife Agencies and Missouri Department of Conservation, 2010).

Although prices that trappers receive for their pelts are a strong determinant of harvest, other factors likely have played a role in fur harvest trends. The number of people choosing to trap has declined in recent years (Organ and others 2001) and likely reflects an overall declining trend in outdoor activities that are linked to wildlife resources (Mockrin and others 2012) among an aging and more urban/suburban dwelling public. Furthermore, there have been efforts by some segments of society to prohibit trapping (Andelt and others 1999). The cumulative effect of these factors has been to reduce the harvest of furbearers in recent years with attendant increases in wildlife damage complaints and concern for disease transmission to humans (Conover 2001; Organ and others 2001; Southwick and others 2005; Levi and others 2012). Recent research has shown that negative opinions about trapping are decreasing (Duda and others 2010), and this may reflect increasing incidence of wildlife damage to personal property and concern for human health. In the absence of economic incentives (increasing pelt prices), it seems likely that the public will bear an increasing proportion of the costs associated with the control of furbearer populations.

Nongame

The nongame category is far and away the most species-rich wildlife group considered in this assessment. Of the more than 148,000 described animal species occurring in the United States (Stein and others 2000a), only a very small percentage are actively managed for recreational or subsistence harvest. Unfortunately, data from which to evaluate status and trends among the species composing this wildlife group are limited to a few taxa (Flather and Sieg 2000) and in some cases are restricted to case studies of a particular population threat. In admitting these data limitations we are simply acknowledging that our evaluation of nongame wildlife cannot be regarded as representative of this group as a whole. Rather, the results presented here simply reflect case examples among those species where some broadly scaled (in time and space) data do exist.

Breeding birds

Birds have long been thought to be good indicators of landscape change, and there is substantial literature documenting how changes in habitat affect the abundance and diversity of bird species that occupy a particular region (Flather 1996; Flather and Sauer 1996; Donovan and Flather 2002; Pidgeon and others 2007; Lepczyk and others 2008). One of the factors contributing to the value of birds as sentinels of important habitat changes is the availability of temporally and geographically extensive monitoring data.

Long-term abundance trends (1966-2008)—Among the 426 species with sufficient data to estimate nationwide trends, 45 percent were found to have stable abundances over the more than 40-year period. The percent of species with declining trends (31 percent) exceeded the percent of species with increasing trends (24 percent). Regionally, the North had the greatest percentage of species with declining trends (32 percent), followed by the Pacific Coast (30 percent), the South (25 percent), and the Rocky Mountain region (19 percent) (Figure 18). The Rocky Mountain and Pacific Coast regions were characterized by the majority of their species showing stable abundance trends (57 percent and 52 percent, respectively).

Among the 12 bird groups examined (Figure 18; Table 5), those with the greatest proportion of declining species include those that nest in and around human settlement (62 percent), nest on or near the ground (49 percent), nest in grassland habitats (44 percent), or nest in shrubland habitats (43 percent). Given that urban land has been increasing (Wear 2011), the high number of urban-associated species with declining abundance is surprising and is likely attributed to methodological artifacts—namely, as urban land encroaches on BBS routes, increased traffic noise makes it more difficult to detect species and ultimately requires relocation of routes away from urbanizing areas (U.S. Geological Survey 2007). Of the five habitat affinity bird groups, those associated with wetland habitats showed the most encouraging results, perhaps because of the prominence wetland habitat has had in the social consciousness over the past few decades and the concurrent efforts to conserve wetland habitats (see Gutzwiller and Flather 2011). Wetland habitat has the lowest percentage of its birds in decline, with nearly 10 percent more species showing long-term population increases than population declines. Notwithstanding these increasing trends in wetland-associated species, there is concern that the recent Supreme Court rulings excluding isolated wetlands from federal regulation may lead to loss or degradation of wetland habitats in the future (Leibowitz 2003; Tiner 2003; Zinn and Copeland 2006). The only other species group with a notable differential between the percentage of increasers relative to decreasers was cavity nesters (32 percent increasing compared to 17 percent decreasing)—a pattern that may be driven by the increasing area of forest habitat in older age classes and increasing area subject to some form of disturbance (USDA 2011: II–7; II–47-48) including fire (Saab and Powell 2005) and insect outbreaks (Klenner and Arsenault 2009; Drever and Martin 2010). Unlike the findings from the 2000 RPA Assessment (*cf.* Flather and others 1999:44), findings of this assessment suggest a differential response among species with different migratory strategies. Nearly 40 percent of neotropical and short-distance migrants showed evidence of significant declining abundances compared to only 24 percent of those species that are permanent residents.

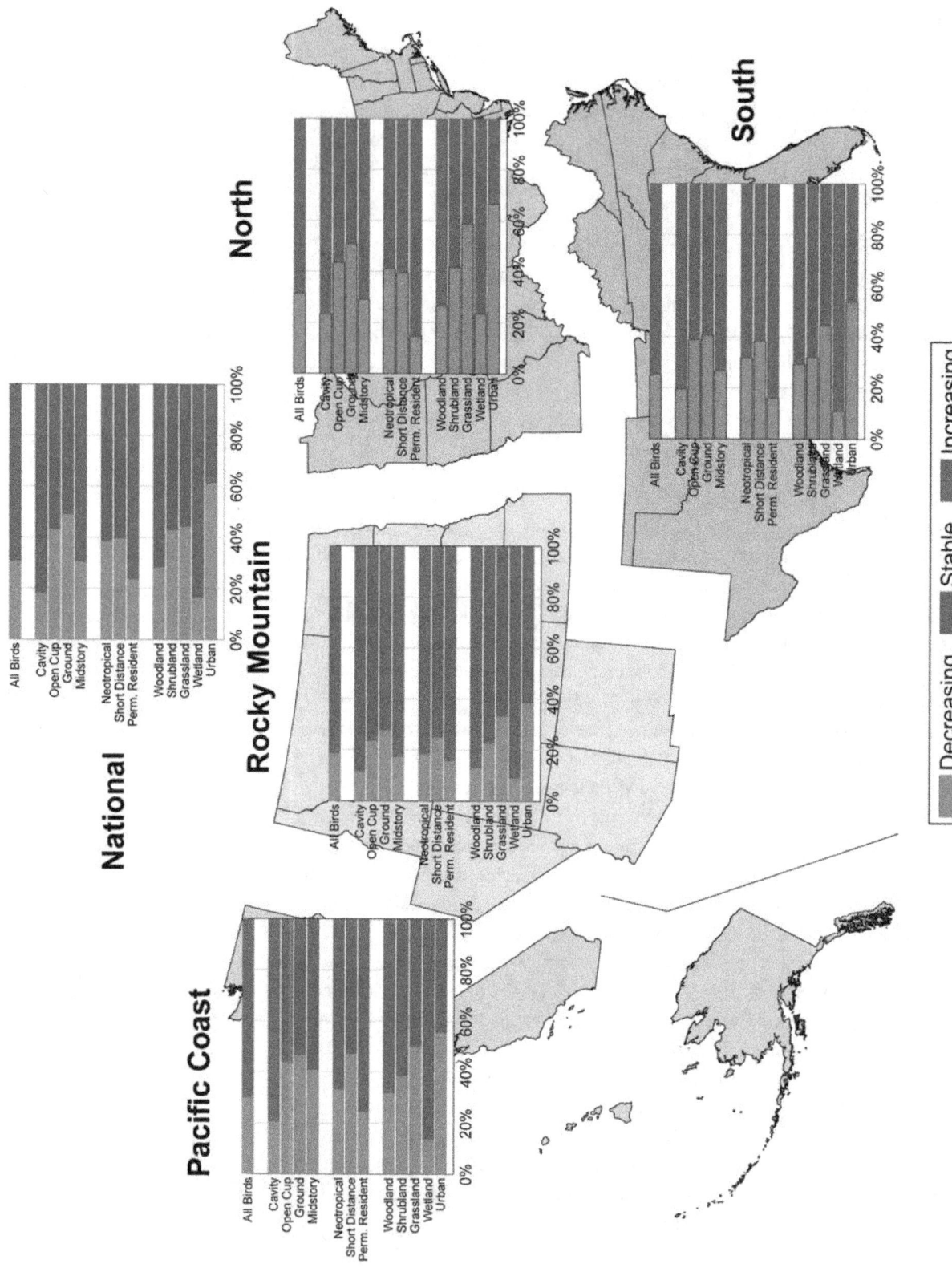

Figure 18—The proportion of bird species (by broad life-history groupings) with decreasing, stable, and increasing trends from 1966 to 2008 for the nation and by RPA region. Species were counted as increasing or decreasing if the trend was different from 0 at $P<0.05$ (source: J. R. Sauer, personal communication, U.S. Geological Survey, Biological Resources Division, Patuxent Wildlife Research Center, 2010).

Table 5—Number of breeding bird species with increasing, decreasing, and stable trends from 1966 to 2008 by life-history characteristics for the United States and RPA Assessment regions. Life history groups are not mutually exclusive or exhaustive and therefore do not sum to the total number of species (J. R. Sauer, personal communication, U.S. Geological Survey, Biological Resources Division, Patuxent Wildlife Research Center, 2010).

Species Group	U.S. Total Species	U.S. Increasing Species %	U.S. Decreasing Species %	U.S. Stable Species %	North Total Species	North Increasing Species %	North Decreasing Species %	North Stable Species %	South Total Species	South Increasing Species %	South Decreasing Species %	South Stable Species %
All Species	426	24.2	30.8	45.1	256	33.6	31.6	34.8	264	27.3	25.0	47.7
Nest type/location												
Cavity	60	31.7	18.3	50.0	30	53.3	23.3	23.3	31	45.2	19.4	35.5
Open cup	178	21.3	43.3	35.4	113	27.4	43.4	29.2	103	22.3	38.8	38.8
Ground/low	110	18.2	49.1	32.7	65	21.5	50.8	27.7	64	14.1	40.6	45.3
Midstory/canopy	121	27.3	30.6	42.1	79	44.3	29.1	26.6	75	36.0	26.7	37.3
Migration status												
Neotropical	137	21.9	38.7	39.4	90	32.2	41.1	26.7	91	19.8	31.9	48.4
Short distance	101	25.7	39.6	34.7	66	36.4	39.4	24.2	60	31.7	38.3	30.0
Permanent resident	88	25.0	23.9	51.1	34	47.1	14.7	38.2	50	36.0	16.0	48.0
Breeding habitat												
Woodland	130	28.5	28.5	43.1	83	42.2	26.5	31.3	65	27.7	29.2	43.1
Shrubland	84	15.5	42.9	41.7	36	19.4	41.7	38.9	50	28.0	32.0	40.0
Grassland	27	11.1	44.4	44.4	17	17.6	58.8	23.5	18	11.1	44.4	44.4
Wetland/open water	84	26.2	16.7	57.1	64	23.4	23.4	53.1	55	23.6	10.9	65.5
Urban	13	23.1	61.5	15.4	12	33.3	66.7	0.0	13	30.8	53.8	15.4
Weighted Mean %		24.4	38.3	42.6		36.1	39.7	33.2		29.0	33.9	44.7

Species Group	Rocky Mountain Total Species	Rocky Mountain Increasing Species %	Rocky Mountain Decreasing Species %	Rocky Mountain Stable Species %	Pacific Coast Total Species	Pacific Coast Increasing Species %	Pacific Coast Decreasing Species %	Pacific Coast Stable Species %
All Species	337	24.3	18.7	57.0	269	17.5	30.1	52.4
Nest type/location								
Cavity	51	35.3	11.8	52.9	43	18.6	20.9	60.5
Open cup	140	24.3	23.6	52.1	101	14.9	43.6	41.6
Ground/low	90	23.3	27.8	48.9	60	11.7	46.7	41.7
Midstory/canopy	97	30.9	17.5	51.5	78	19.2	41.0	39.7
Migration status								
Neotropical	108	27.8	18.5	53.7	72	16.7	33.3	50.0
Short distance	92	22.8	25.0	52.2	70	20.0	47.1	32.9
Permanent resident	70	24.3	15.7	60.0	65	18.5	24.6	56.9
Breeding habitat								
Woodland	99	32.3	13.1	54.5	75	21.3	32.0	46.7
Shrubland	70	22.9	22.9	54.3	57	8.8	38.6	52.6
Grassland	27	14.8	33.3	51.9	12	0.0	50.0	50.0
Wetland/open water	65	21.5	9.2	69.2	59	16.9	13.6	69.5
Urban	13	7.7	38.5	53.8	9	22.2	55.6	22.2
Weighted Mean %		26.8	22.0	54.7		17.6	39.0	49.9

Regional patterns of abundance trends among bird groups did indicate that regions characterized by prominent human impacts tended to have higher proportions of declining species (Table 5). Weighted mean percentages across bird groups indicated that the North had the highest percentage of declining species on average (40 percent), followed closely by the Pacific Coast (39 percent). The South had an average decline among bird groups of 34 percent. The Rocky Mountain region had the lowest mean percentage of declining species (22 percent), and it was the only region where the mean percentage of increasing species (27 percent) exceeded the percentage of declining species.

Abundance trends since the last assessment (1997-2008)—The 2000 RPA Assessment (*cf.* Flather and others 1999) reported on bird abundance trends through 1996. Estimation of trends over the 1997 to 2008 period gave us an opportunity to see if recent trends were consistent with long-term trends. Because the trend is being estimated over a shorter temporal window, detection of significant trends is less likely. For this reason it is not surprising that all bird groups showed greater percentages of species with stable abundance trends than was observed over the longer term (Table 6). Unlike the long-term trends, there was a higher percentage of species with increasing trends (28 percent) relative to decreasing trends (18 percent).

Among the 12 bird life-history groups, there were 6 groups where the percentage of species with increasing trends exceeded the percentage with decreasing trends—compared to only 2 groups in the longer term. These results suggest that in the shorter term, bird abundance trends have been dominated by species with stable to increasing trends since 1997. However, it is noteworthy that species associated with urban habitats, grassland habitats, and those that nest on or near the ground showed abundance trends that were consistent with the long-term patterns—namely, strong evidence that these species groups have continued to decline in the near term (Table 6). This latter pattern has prompted some to label the noted long-term declines among species associated with grass-shrub habitats as one of the prominent conservation crises of the 21st century (Brennan and Kuvlesky 2005).

Recent regional bird abundance trends tended to be consistent with the national pattern. The majority of all bird species, estimated as weighted mean percentages across the 12 bird groups, had stable abundance trends in all RPA regions except the North (Table 6). Furthermore, the mean percentage of species with increasing trends exceeded the percentage of species with declining trends in all regions except the Pacific Coast where the percent of species declining exceeded the percent increasing by 7 percentage points (Table 6). These near-term trends among regions also suggest that the last decade has been characterized by conditions leading to stable to increasing abundance trends.

Table 6—Number of breeding bird species with increasing, decreasing, and stable trends from 1997 to 2008 by life-history characteristics for the total United States and RPA Assessment regions. Life history groups are not mutually exclusive or exhaustive and therefore do not sum to the total number of species (J. R. Sauer, personal communication, U.S. Geological Survey, Biological Resources Division, Patuxent Wildlife Research Center, 2010).

	Total U.S.				North				South			
	Total	Increasing Species	Decreasing Species	Stable Species	Total	Increasing Species	Decreasing Species	Stable Species	Total	Increasing Species	Decreasing Species	Stable Species
		%	%	%		%	%	%				
All Species	426	27.9	18.1	54.0	256	28.1	20.7	51.2	264	26.9	12.1	61.0
Nest type/location												
Cavity	60	36.7	8.3	55.0	30	50.0	16.7	33.3	31	45.2	3.2	51.6
Open cup	178	24.7	27.5	47.8	113	23.0	31.0	46.0	103	21.4	22.3	56.3
Ground/low	110	19.1	30.9	50.0	65	21.5	33.8	44.6	64	17.2	21.9	60.9
Midstory/canopy	121	32.2	19.0	48.8	79	32.9	24.1	43.0	75	33.3	14.7	52.0
Migration status												
Neotropical	137	33.6	19.7	46.7	90	27.8	24.4	47.8	91	25.3	14.3	60.4
Short distance	101	26.7	29.7	43.6	66	27.3	36.4	36.4	60	26.7	25.0	48.3
Permanent resident	88	23.9	12.5	63.6	34	38.2	11.8	50.0	50	28.0	6.0	66.0
Breeding habitat												
Woodland	130	34.6	16.2	49.2	83	32.5	20.5	47.0	65	32.3	9.2	58.5
Shrubland	84	20.2	21.4	58.3	36	19.4	27.8	52.8	50	20.0	16.0	64.0
Grassland	27	25.9	29.6	44.4	17	23.5	41.2	35.3	18	11.1	16.7	72.2
Wetland/open water	84	23.8	8.3	67.9	64	21.9	6.3	71.9	55	25.5	3.6	70.9
Urban	13	23.1	53.8	23.1	12	33.3	58.3	8.3	13	23.1	53.8	23.1
Weighted Mean %		28.7	24.3	52.4		29.7	29.4	48.8		27.7	20.6	59.5

	Rocky Mountain				Pacific Coast			
Species Group	Total Species	Increasing Species	Decreasing Species	Stable Species	Total Species	Increasing Species	Decreasing Species	Stable Species
		%	%	%		%	%	%
All Species	337	22.8	11.9	65.3	269	13.8	15.6	70.6
Nest type/location								
Cavity	51	27.5	3.9	68.6	43	14.0	11.6	74.4
Open cup	140	23.6	16.4	60.0	101	11.9	22.8	65.3
Ground/low	90	16.7	16.7	66.7	60	8.3	28.3	63.3
Midstory/canopy	97	30.9	13.4	55.7	78	16.7	19.2	64.1
Migration status								
Neotropical	108	29.6	8.3	62.0	72	13.9	19.4	66.7
Short distance	92	19.6	16.3	64.1	70	14.3	25.7	60.0
Permanent resident	70	22.9	11.4	65.7	65	12.3	10.8	76.9
Breeding habitat								
Woodland	99	30.3	6.1	63.6	75	18.7	13.3	68.0
Shrubland	70	20.0	17.1	62.9	57	8.8	19.3	71.9
Grassland	27	18.5	22.2	59.3	12	0.0	33.3	66.7
Wetland/open water	65	16.9	7.7	75.4	59	15.3	5.1	79.7
Urban	13	15.4	30.8	53.8	9	0.0	33.3	66.7
Weighted Mean %		25.0	14.9	63.7		14.2	21.2	68.8

Amphibians

Within the United States there are just over 300 species of amphibians (198 salamanders and 103 frogs and toads) (NatureServe 2010, 2011)—an increase of about 70 species since the 2000 RPA Assessment. These increases are undoubtedly due to taxonomic refinements with the advent of molecular techniques to distinguish species in evolutionarily complex groups (Flather and others 2004). Conservation concern for this taxonomic group first began to surface at the First World Congress of Herpetology back in 1989. Many of the early reports at that time documented local and regional amphibian declines in both human disturbed and pristine habitats (see Blaustein and Wake 1990) suggesting that declines were widespread. There long has been agreement that habitat destruction and other human-related disturbances can result in local population declines or extirpations (Pechmann and Wilbur 1994). However, the absence of spatially and temporally extensive monitoring data severely limited the ability of conservation science to determine if these reported declines reflected a widespread pattern of population degradation (Stuart and others 2004). Furthermore, large natural population fluctuations among some amphibians further confounded unequivocal determination of cause and geographic scope associated with these noted declines (Pechmann and others 1991; Hecnar and M'Closkey 1996; Raithel and others 2011). Naturally fluctuating populations and the dearth of geographically widespread and long-term surveys together made assessing the status of amphibians one of the more controversial topics in conservation biology in the early 1990s (Reed and Blaustein 1995).

One of the early attempts to compile status evaluations from professional herpetologists over large geographic areas was included in a report from the Declining Amphibian Populations Task Force. Vial and Saylor (1993), who summarized the findings of this early compilation, identified a total of 120 amphibian species or subspecies of conservation concern[6] in the continental United States, and their listing is included in the 2000 RPA Assessment (Flather and others 1999:52). A simple tally of species (or subspecies) by RPA region based on state-level occurrence information provided by Vial and Saylor (1993) indicated that the greatest number of amphibians of conservation concern occurred in the Pacific Coast region, followed by the North, Rocky Mountain, and the South regions (Table 7). The number of genera represented among the species or subspecies of conservation concern was greatest in the North followed in rank order by the South/Pacific Coast (tied) and the Rocky Mountains. Because this synthesis was based on combining results from independent local studies, it lacked the rigor that could have been achieved had regional or national monitoring protocols been in place. Therefore, the patterns summarized in the 2000 RPA Assessment were viewed as tentative.

In an effort to gauge how the distribution of amphibians of conservation concern by RPA region may have changed since the Vial and Saylor (1993) compilation was reported in the 2000 RPA Assessment, we used NatureServe (2010, 2011) occurrence records to judge the

---

[6] Species of conservation concern were defined as those species (or subspecies) with the following status categories: population decline observed, federal or state threatened and endangered species, federal candidate species, rare, sensitive, regional concern, state species of special concern, state critical, state vulnerable, candidate for state status, or locally absent. Species with International Union for the Conservation of Nature and Natural Resources (IUCN) categories of extinct, extinct in the wild, critical, endangered, vulnerable, and susceptible were also included.

Table 7—Number of amphibians of conservation concern as determined by various criteria. Rank of each RPA region within criterion is shown parenthetically.

Criteria for determining species of conservation concern	Taxa tallied	RPA region			
		North	South	Rocky Mountain	Pacific Coast
Vial and Saylor (1993)	Species/subspecies	42 (2)	26 (4)	39 (3)	51 (1)
	Genera	17 (1)	14 (2)	12 (3)	14 (2)
NatureServe (2010, 2011)	Species	6 (4)	70 (1)	11 (3)	41 (2)
Global Ranks	Genera	4 (4)	14 (1)	6 (3)	10 (2)
NatureServe (2010, 2011)	Species/subspecies	76 (2)	175 (1)	67 (3)	67 (3)
Global Ranks, State Ranks	Genera	20 (2)	31 (1)	20 (2)	16 (3)

current distribution of amphibians considered to be at risk of extinction (G1-G3 conservation ranks as defined in Table 3). If we restrict our tally to full species, then NatureServe identifies 123 amphibian species considered to be at risk of extinction. Given that the South is considered a hotspot of salamander diversification and endemism (IUCN 2011), it was not surprising that this region was ranked highest in the number of species and genera (70 species; 14 genera) considered to be at risk of extinction (Table 7). Although the Pacific Coast region does not share the same degree of amphibian diversity as the South (Ricketts and others 1999), it ranks second in amphibian species and genera counts that are at risk (Table 7). The more arid ecosystems of the Rocky Mountain region support fewer amphibians and the counts of species and genera of concern were lower there, but it was somewhat surprising that this region did not rank lowest in at-risk amphibian counts because of the general depauperate nature of the amphibian fauna. The lowest count was actually observed in the North (Table 7) even though amphibian diversity among the ecoregions that compose the North rank second to the South (see Ricketts and others 1999).

If we relax the criteria for defining amphibians of conservation concern to include those species (and subspecies) that were determined to be of conservation concern at the state level (SX, SH, S1-S3)—criteria that were more consistent with those used in Vial and Saylor (1993)—then the RPA regional rankings shift substantially (Table 7). A total of 302 species (or subspecies) were determined to be of concern—about 2.5 times the number of species (or subspecies) that were originally tallied by Vial and Saylor (1993). The South continued to rank highest in the number of species and genera of conservation concern, but the North ranked second in species (or subspecies) and tied for second with the Rocky Mountain region in number of genera (Table 7). The fact that the North has a high number of species/subspecies under these criteria and ranked lowest when using global ranks among full species suggests that amphibian populations may be threatened locally in the North but secure elsewhere within their geographic range.

The monitoring component of ARMI has accumulated a total of 118 time series since 2002 (see Adams and others 2012). Individual estimates of species occupancy among 39 monitoring areas distributed across the coterminous United States indicated that the probability of site occupancy among 50 species has declined, on average, by 4.5 percent annually over the

2002-2011 period. Although the occupancy trends among the individual species vary, nearly 62 percent (73 of 118 time series) showed evidence of a declining trend within the 2002-2011 period. Interpretation of these broad occupancy trends across the coterminous United States must be done cautiously for a number of reasons. First, much of the noted occupancy decline since 2002 can be attributed to a relatively high initial proportional occupancy rate in 2002 (~0.65) that was based on fewer than 30 individual occupancy estimates. Although the number of annual occupancy estimates has grown since 2002—reaching a maximum of ~90 in 2005 and 2006—the proportional occupancy estimates have remained relatively stable (~0.50) since 2003. Secondly, the primary objective of ARMI is to provide resource managers with local information concerning occupancy trends, habitat relationships, and responses to natural or human-induced environmental change (Adams and others 2012). The 39 monitoring sites making up the ARMI were selected for various reasons, raising questions about their representativeness in deriving unbiased inferences across broad geographic extents (http://armi.usgs.gov/wch.php#1).

The threats implicated in the elevated concern for amphibian conservation are numerous and multifaceted (Beebee and Griffiths 2005). Factors that had been identified in the 2000 RPA Assessment as key in several population declines included direct habitat destruction or contamination (Petranka and others 1993; Hecnar and M'Closkey 1996); acidification (Dunson and others 1992; Wissinger and Whiteman 1992); elevated ultraviolet-B radiation resulting from anthropogenic ozone depletion (Blaustein and others 1994a); introduced predators (for example, bullfrogs and fish) (Fisher and Shaffer 1996); and pathogens (Blaustein and others 1994b). Furthermore, amphibians possess multiple traits associated with high susceptibility to climate change including specialized habitat requirements, dependence on specific environmental cues that could be disrupted by climate change, and poor dispersal ability (Walther and others 2002; Foden and others 2009; Lawler and others 2009). However, after the discovery of the fungal disease chytridiomycosis (caused by the chytrid fungus) in the late 1990s, this pathogen along with other emerging infectious diseases including amphibian ranaviruses, a fungal-like oomycetes (*Saprolegnia ferax*), and a digenetic trematode (*Ribeiroia ondatrae*), have become some of the most worrying threats given their association with mass mortality events (Beebee and Griffiths 2005; Gray and others 2009; Kiesecker 2011; Ohmer and Bishop 2011). Still other researchers are proposing complex interactive effects among these agents and other stressors, including climate change and human population densities (Long and others 1995; Murray and others 2011; Rohr and others 2011). What seems almost a certainty now is that many factors are contributing to amphibian population declines, and the relative importance of each factor will vary considerably among species, regions, and microclimates (Beebee and Griffiths 2005; Bradford 2005; Hof and others 2011). Furthermore, it is equally certain that detecting cases of decline and determining causation will require rigorous long-term monitoring and experimental manipulation (Blaustein 1994; Beebee and Griffiths 2005; Kiesecker 2011).

Bats

There are approximately 45 species of bats that occur in the United States, of which 7 species or subspecies are currently listed as threatened or endangered under the Endangered Species Act of 1973 (http://ecos.fws.gov/tess_public/). Like many species with secretive and cryptic habits, bat populations lack associated monitoring data that would permit broad-scale assessment of population status (O'Shea and others 2003). In the absence of rigorously designed monitoring programs, conservation scientists and managers often rely on meta-analytic approaches to summarize across existing local monitoring efforts. Such was the approach taken by Ellison and others (2003) who compiled a central database to store estimates of colony size at winter and summer roost sites that appeared in the peer-reviewed literature, theses and dissertations, unpublished technical reports, or monitoring records maintained by federal, state, conservation resource groups, or individual researchers. Of the colony estimates from 6,044 unique roost locations gathered by Ellison and others (2003), we used data from 293 hibernacula and 151 summer roosts (including maternity, bachelor, transient, and colonies of an unspecified function) occurring in the United States that each had at least four years of colony size estimates. Although the monitoring time periods varied, most colony counts were conducted after 1980, and the most recent counts occurred in 2000.

Among the 293 winter roost counts, the majority (67 percent) showed no evidence of a trend; 19 percent indicated increasing colony size; and 14 percent were classified as declining. One third of the hibernacula counts of more than four years were focused on the Indiana bat due to its long-term conservation interest as one of the first species listed as endangered, in 1967. Nearly 31 percent of winter roost trend analyses were determined to be declining while 19 percent were determined to be increasing.

Summer roost counts were more temporally variable and, as such, were less likely to show a detectable trend. Of the 151 summer roost counts of four or more years, 84 percent showed no evidence of a trend, with the remaining counts being nearly equally split between increasing (9 percent) and declining (7 percent) (Ellison and others 2003:136). Like the hibernacula counts, summer counts were concentrated on another endangered species—the gray bat, which was added to the list in 1976. Unlike in the Indiana bat winter roost counts, Ellison and others (2003) found that only 6 percent of gray bat summer roost counts showed evidence of decline and more than 86 percent had no detectable trend.

The distribution of summer and winter roost counts varied greatly among RPA regions (Figure 19). The eastern United States is where most of the roost counts of four or more years were concentrated, with 51 percent in the North and 38 percent in the South. The western United States has received far fewer roost counts, with 9 percent in the Rocky Mountain region and 2 percent in the Pacific Coast. Among hibernacula counts, the greatest percent with evidence of declining trends occurred in the South (18 percent), whereas the North had the greatest percent with evidence of increasing trends (26 percent). The absence of any evidence indicating a trend dominates the summer roost counts in all RPA regions (Figure 19). Again, the North had the greatest percentage of summer counts with increasing trends (11 percent), while the Rocky Mountain region had the greatest percentage of summer counts with declining trends (11 percent). However, we caution that patterns observed among roost counts in the West may not be representative of bat population trends region-wide, given the few number of counts that were available for analysis.

Although the data compiled by Ellison and others (2003) reflects the dedicated efforts among biologists to monitor a species that provides substantial ecological services (consumption of insect pests) to the agricultural and forestry sectors of the economy (see Boyles and others

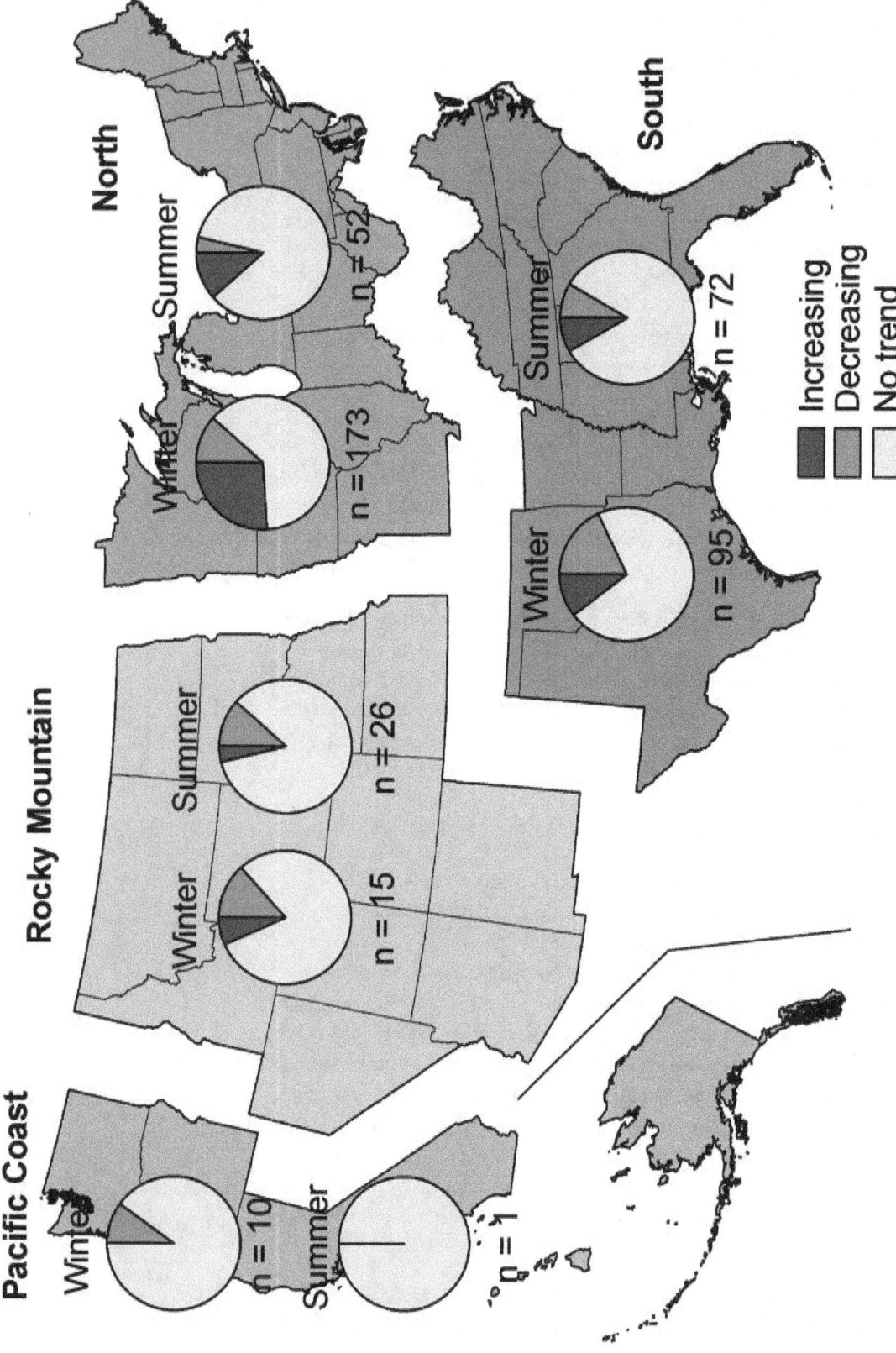

Figure 19—The proportion of colony (winter and summer) counts with at least 4 years of survey effort that were determined by Ellison and others (2003) to show evidence of increasing, decreasing, or no trend in bat numbers by RPA region.

2011; Kunz and others 2011), the lack of standardized reporting, incomplete descriptions of how the counts were conducted, and the uncertainty associated with using roost counts to reflect population status highlight the difficulty in using existing and highly variable data to evaluate broad-scale trends among species with complex and diverse life histories (O'Shea and others 2003). Consequently, the results reviewed here provide only a glimpse of the kind of broad-scale analyses and questions that could be addressed with rigorously designed bat monitoring schemes. As noted by O'Shea and others (2003), such schemes will be difficult to develop and implement in the absence of firmer mandates for bat conservation. Calls for stronger bat conservation and monitoring may be on the horizon, given the elevated and substantial bat mortality attributed to the aforementioned white-nose syndrome—an emerging disease linked with catastrophic population collapse among bat hibernacula in the northeastern United States (Blehert and others 2009).

White-nose syndrome, a most-often fatal disease of bats, is characterized by the visible presence of white fungus on bats' muzzles, ears, and wing membranes. First observed in the winter of 2006-2007 in caves and mines in upstate New York, it is thought to be caused by a recently identified fungus *(Geomyces destructans)* (Gargas and others 2009; Lorch and others 2011), which thrives in the low temperatures and high humidity of many bat hibernacula. Blehert and others (2009) found hibernacula losses that sometimes exceeded 75 percent, while Reichard and Kunz (2009) found that colonies in some hibernacula almost entirely disappeared. A consistent behavioral pattern that has been observed in bats with white-nose syndrome is abnormally high number of arousals from hibernation or abnormally long arousals. This greater than normal winter activity depletes fat reserves in the infected bats, which leads to a host of health problems. However, it is unknown whether these winter-flying bats are seeking food or water, and the ultimate cause of death is not fully understood.

Cryan and others (2010) found that the fungus affects the skin membranes of bats, particularly on the wings, damaging the wings themselves and causing them to tear easily and lose their tensile strength and elasticity. They also found evidence that the fungus impairs the blood flow throughout the wings, even though the fungus is not vasculotropic—that is, does not directly invade the blood vessels. It is thought that the wing membrane damage, in turn, impairs the ability for the bat to regulate its water balance.

Thus far, seven species of bats are known to be affected: the little brown bat, Indiana bat, northern long-eared bat, eastern small-footed bat, tricolored bat, big brown bat, and the gray bat (USDI, Fish and Wildlife Service 2011, 2012). Whatever the cause of the mortality associated with white-nose syndrome, its spread has been alarming (Figure 20). White-nose syndrome was first found in Schoharie County, New York, and by the following year was found in many hibernacula of New York, but was also found as far away as southern Virginia. It then spread northwest into Ontario, Canada, as well as throughout the karst topography of the Appalachians. The following year saw the spread of the disease into the far north of New Brunswick and Nova Scotia, continued infilling of the Appalachians, and some spread south and west. The disease is now concentrated in a band along the Appalachians and in several outlying spots, including Oklahoma, Missouri, and eastern Virginia.

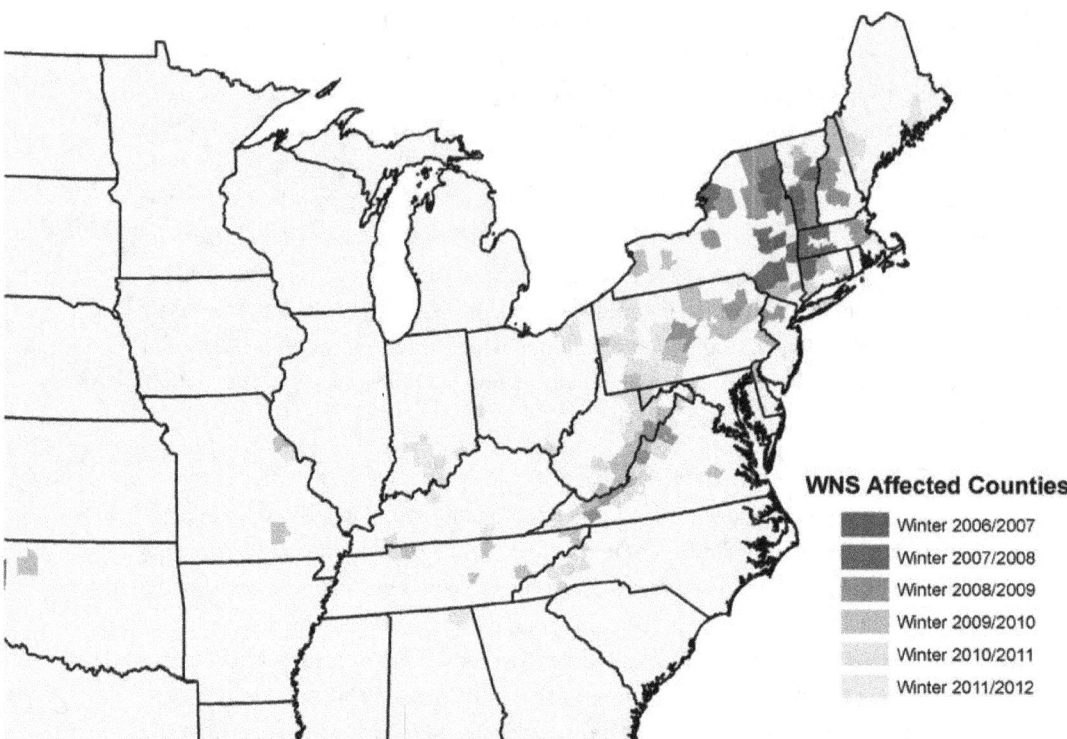

Figure 20—County-level incidence of white-nose syndrome (suspected or confirmed) since its discovery in 2006 (source: Bat Conservation International, http://www.batcon.org/index.php/what-we-do/white-nose-syndrome/).

In response to white-nose syndrome and its associated high mortality among bats, the U.S. Fish and Wildlife Service, with participation from many other federal agencies and state and tribal agencies, including the U.S. Forest Service, the Bureau of Land Management, the U.S. Geological Survey, and the National Park Service, is developing a national response plan (USDI, Fish and Wildlife Service 2011). The plan is intended to assist state, federal, and tribal agencies in managing bat populations threatened by white-nose syndrome.

Pollinators

Plant-pollinator interactions are among the most important and best-known ecosystem services supplied by managed and free-living wild organisms. It has been estimated that more than 87 percent of the world's flowering plants are pollinated by animals—a percentage that is slightly reduced to 78 percent in temperate-zone ecosystems (Ollerton and others 2011). Recent value estimates of pollination services to the U.S. agricultural sector range from $3.1 billion attributed to native free-living pollinators (almost exclusively bees) to $16.4 billion attributed to the European honey bee (estimates in 2003 dollars; Morse and Calderone 2000; Losey and Vaughan 2006). Because of the magnitude of these economic values and the accumulating evidence of local and regional declines, concern for reductions in pollinator biodiversity, both in terms of abundance and variety of organisms, has grown in recent decades (Kremen and others 2007). Unfortunately, for most pollinator species occurring in the United States, long-term population monitoring data are very limited (National Research Council 2007) making it difficult, if not controversial (see Ghazoul 2005a, b; Steffan-Dewenter and others 2005), to evaluate the status and trends of this functionally important group of animals.

Status and trend data are most well developed for honey bee populations because management of honey bees to provide pollination services as well as agricultural commodities is a well-developed discipline (National Research Council 2007). There is little contention that the decline in honey bee colony numbers has been substantial. Data from the USDA National Agricultural Statistics Service show that since 1947 there has been a 59 percent decline in the number of colonies producing honey (National Research Council 2007). Furthermore, there is evidence that many feral honey bee colonies have undergone local extinction, often leaving beekeepers as the only source for honey bees on the landscape (Potts and others 2010).

Assessing the wild pollinators is more difficult given the paucity of long-term monitoring data and the fragmentary nature of more locally scaled investigations available to assess population trends (National Research Council 2007). Efforts to synthesize local-scaled efforts do suggest that there has been widespread loss of pollinator abundance and richness that may be focused on those species with more specialized diets and habitats (Potts and others 2010). Such syntheses also seem to be supported by studies specifically designed to explore broad-scale patterns. In particular, Cameron and others (2011) found that among eight species of bumble bees distributed throughout North America, four showed declines in relative abundance of up to 96 percent. Factors that have been implicated in the widespread declines of insect pollinators include parasitic mites, pathogens, invasive species, agricultural intensification, competition with introduced pollinators, and habitat loss (National Research Council 2007). One of the concerning emergent effects of pollinator declines is elevated coextinction among members of co-evolved systems, of which plant-pollinator relationships is a prime example (Wiens and Slaton 2012). Analyses conducted for previous RPA Assessments (Flather and others 1994; Flather and others 1998) have observed evidence legitimizing such concerns among the endangered biota concentrated in southern California—a region where many recent insect extinctions are thought to have occurred (Pyle and others 1981).

Monitoring data among avian pollinators over broad spatial extents and long time periods were more readily available through the BBS. Data on eight species of hummingbirds were sufficient to estimate both long- (1966-2008) and short-term (1997-2008) trends. However, trends in hummingbird relative abundance must be interpreted cautiously since they are more difficult to detect with the BBS because they are not as vocal as other bird species. Among the eight species, three showed evidence of significantly increasing long-term trends, including the ruby-throated, black-chinned, and Anna's hummingbirds; evidence for long-term declines was observed for the broad-tailed, rufous, and Allen's hummingbirds (Figure 21). The patterns of increase and decline in the short term are consistent with the long-term patterns except fewer significant trends were detected. Hummingbird trends did differ regionally, with significant declining trends being restricted to the two western RPA regions (Figure 21).

Hummingbird Species	Long Term 1966-2008					Short Term 1997-2008				
	National	North	South	Rocky Mountain	Pacific Coast	National	North	South	Rocky Mountain	Pacific Coast
Ruby-throated	↗	↗	↗	↗	·	↗	↗	↗	+	·
Black-chinned	↗	·	+	+	+	↗	·	+	↗	+
Costa's	−	·	·	−	+	+	·	·	−	+
Anna's	↗	·	·	↗	↗	+	·	·	+	+
Broad-tailed	↘	·	·	↘	·	−	·	·	−	·
Rufous	↘	·	·	+	↘	↘	·	·	+	↘
Allen's	↘	·	·	·	↘	↘	·	·	·	↘
Calliope	−	·	·	+	−	+	·	·	+	+

Figure 21—Long term (1966-2008) and short term (1997-2008) population trends in selected hummingbird species for the nation and by RPA region from the North American Breeding Bird Survey. Bolded arrows indicate the direction of significant (*P*<0.05) trends; minus (-) and plus (+) signs indicate a trend that was not determined to be significantly different from stable. Missing value entries (•) occur when there was an insufficient sample (species observed on <15 routes) to estimate a trend (source: J.R. Sauer, personal communication, U.S. Geological Survey, Biological Resources Division, Patuxent Wildlife Research Center, 2010).

Imperiled Species and Species of Conservation Concern

In the last decade there has been growing use of ecosystem services to economically justify biodiversity conservation programs that ultimately contribute to human well-being (Fisher and others 2009). One of the outcomes of this shift has been a more comprehensive accounting of how biodiversity benefits human society, including the provision of material goods (timber, food, fiber, and medicines), maintenance of key regulatory functions (flood control, pollination, pest control, climate regulation, nutrient cycling, and carbon sequestration), and a number of amenity or cultural benefits (recreation, spiritual values, cultural heritage, education, and mental health) (Millennium Ecosystem Assessment 2005; Rands and others 2010). Notwithstanding the substantial benefits attributed to biotic resources, the costs associated with biodiversity degradation remain overshadowed by the economic benefits of resource extraction and land use intensification to support growing human populations (Ehrlich and Pringle 2008; Johns 2010; Woodwell 2010). For this reason, recent efforts to conserve biodiversity are seen as largely insufficient to offset human drivers (habitat loss, overexploitation, and invasive exotic species) of increased species rarity and extinction (Butchart and others 2010; Hoffmann and others 2010). Thus, global biodiversity has not only continued to decline (Stokstad 2010) but is declining at an accelerated pace (Mooney and Mace 2009).

Are recent trends in the conservation status of species observed in the United States consistent with this global perspective? Based on data documenting the number and occurrence of species formally listed as threatened or endangered under the ESA, and those considered to be at-risk of extinction based on a broader, and politically buffered, assessment of conservation status under criteria specified by NatureServe, patterns of species imperilment for the United States are generally consistent with the recently noted global patterns. However, the degree to which the biota is imperiled does vary among taxonomic groups and geographically.

ESA listings and at-risk species

As of 27 October 2010, there were a total of 1,368 species formally listed as threatened or endangered within the United States. The pattern of listing has varied over time and has seen shifts in taxonomic focus (Figure 22). If we ignore 181 species that were documented as threatened or endangered with publication of the first Endangered Species Technical Bulletin in July of 1976 (because that number reflects the cumulative number of species that had been listed prior to July of 1976 and those that were initially listed with passage of the Act in 1973), annual listings tended to increase from 1980 through the mid-1990s (Figure 22a), reaching a maximum annual listing of 110 species in 1992. Since 1992 there has been a general decline in annual listings through 2005 when there was no net change in the number of species receiving protection under the ESA. Since 2005 there have been intermittent periods of net gains in listed species.

The 1,368 species receiving protection under the ESA as of 27 October 2010 represented a net gain of 278 species since the 2000 RPA Assessment (Figure 22). Much of the increase in listed species is attributable to gains among plants (+152), fish (+31), insects (+27), mollusks (+20), mammals (+20), and amphibians (+8). Since 1 March 2006, the listing rate has nearly doubled (~23 species/year) over the listing rate observed for the earlier half of the decade (Flather and others 2008)—a listing rate that could be sustained for more than a decade depending on the degree of political support for species listings and how rapidly final determinations are made on species that are proposed (23 species) or candidates[7] (253 species) for listing.

Using NatureServe's criteria as a broader assessment of conservation status revealed that nearly one quarter of all known vertebrates, and more than one third of known invertebrates and vascular plants, are considered at-risk of extinction (Figure 23). Vertebrate species of conservation concern are prominent among amphibians (41 percent), freshwater fishes (37 percent), and reptiles (21 percent)—birds ranked the lowest with 14 percent of the species occurring in the United States assessed to be either at risk of extinction or potentially extinct. Among invertebrates, mollusks (58 percent) and crustaceans (53 percent) had the greatest percentage of known species considered to be of conservation concern. Animal groups associated with aquatic habitats (amphibians, freshwater fish, mollusks, and crustaceans) had higher

---

[7] A proposed species is one for which a proposed rule to list as either threatened or endangered has been formally published in the Federal Register; a candidate for listing is a species for which the U.S. Fish and Wildlife Service has sufficient information on file to support proposals to list the species as threatened or endangered, but for which preparation and publication of a listing proposal is precluded by other listing activities (USDI, Fish and Wildlife Service 1996:7598).

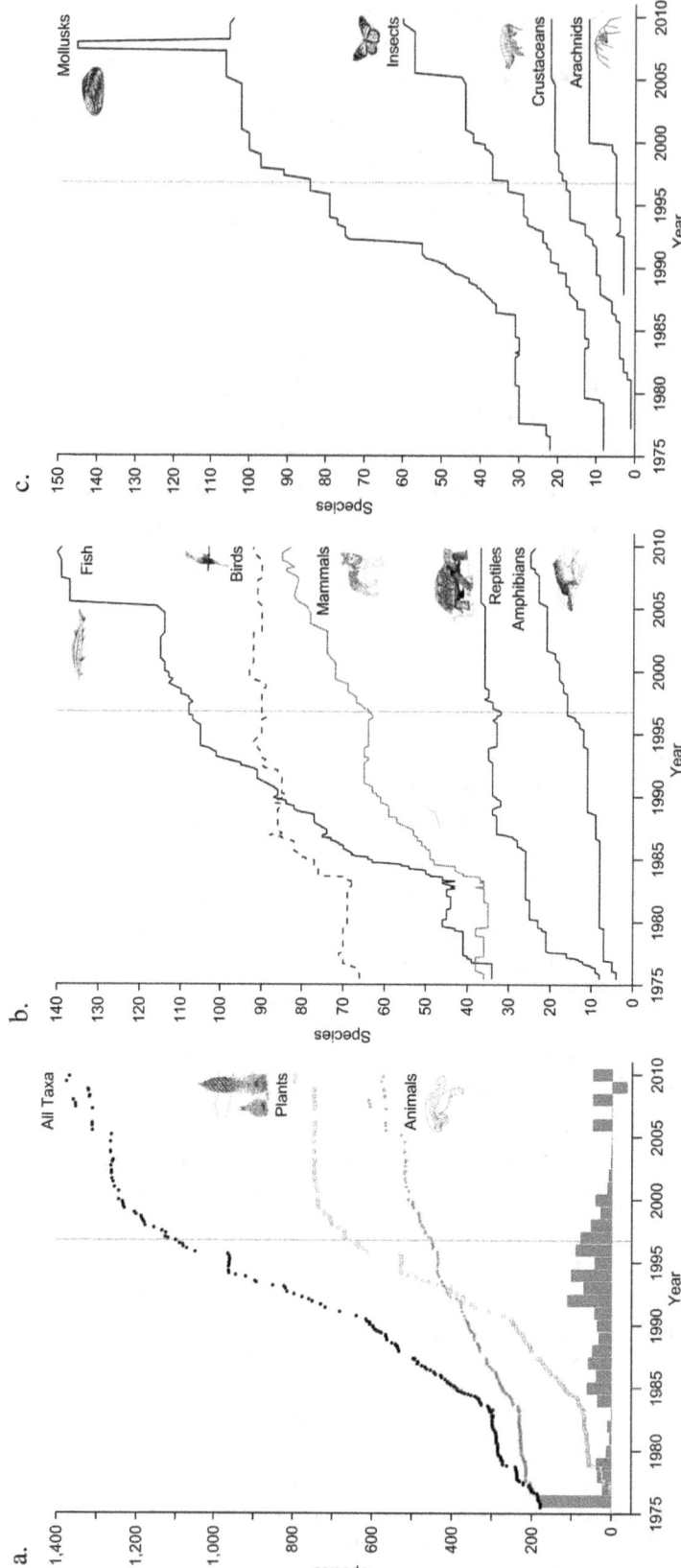

Figure 22—Cumulative number of species listed as threatened or endangered (accounting for delistings) from 1 July 1976 through 27 October 2010 for (a) plants and animals, (b) vertebrate groups, and (c) invertebrate groups. The number of species added in each year is shown by the red bars in (a). The vertical dashed line reflects the date of the data used in the 2000 RPA Assessment (Flather and others 1999). The spike in mussel listings was associated with an accounting change tied to species collectively referenced as Oahu tree snails (*Achatinella* spp.), which is now listed as an endangered genus (M. Bender, personal communication, U.S. Department of the Interior, Fish and Wildlife Service, 3 Aug 2010).

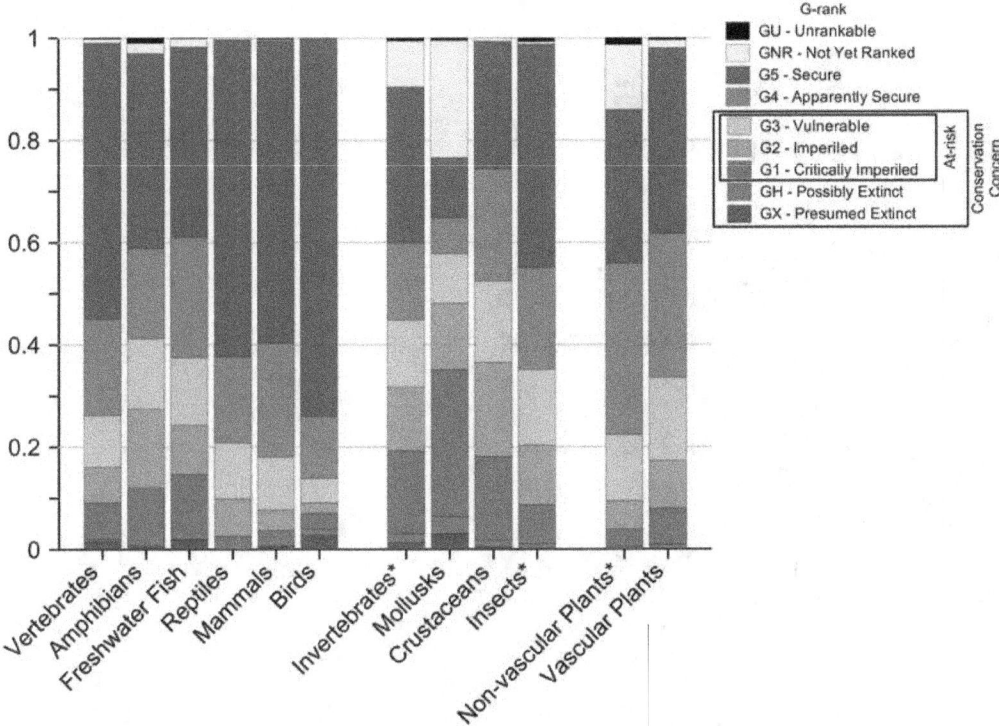

Figure 23—The proportion of species occurring in the United States assigned to each NatureServe conservation status rank for vertebrates, invertebrates, and plants. Asterisks (*) indicate those taxonomic groups with uncertain proportions because many species are awaiting conservation assessments.

proportions of at-risk species (all exceeding 35 percent) than did taxonomic groups more typically associated with terrestrial habitats (reptiles, mammals, and birds), which tended to have less than 20 percent of their species assessed to be at-risk (see also Loftus and Flather 2012). Furthermore, there is evidence that amphibians as a group are underlisted (many more species are considered at-risk than are listed under ESA) and underfunded (per species recovery expenditures are much lower than for terrestrial vertebrates) (Gratwicke and others 2012). Among those species that are associated with forest habitats, the percent of species considered to be at-risk has been growing in the short term—with nearly a 1 percent gain in at-risk species among the relatively well-studied forest-associated vertebrates over a 5-year period from the early- to mid-2000s (Flather and others, in press).

The proportion of species of conservation concern varies among RPA regions (Figure 24). Species of conservation concern make up a relatively high proportion of the biota in the South and Pacific Coast regions, with greater than 20 percent of their vertebrate and nearly 40 percent of their invertebrate faunas being classified as either at-risk or potentially extinct. The North and Rocky Mountain regions show relatively lower degrees of imperilment, with about 10 percent of their vertebrate and from 20 to 30 percent of their invertebrate faunas qualifying as at-risk or potentially extinct.

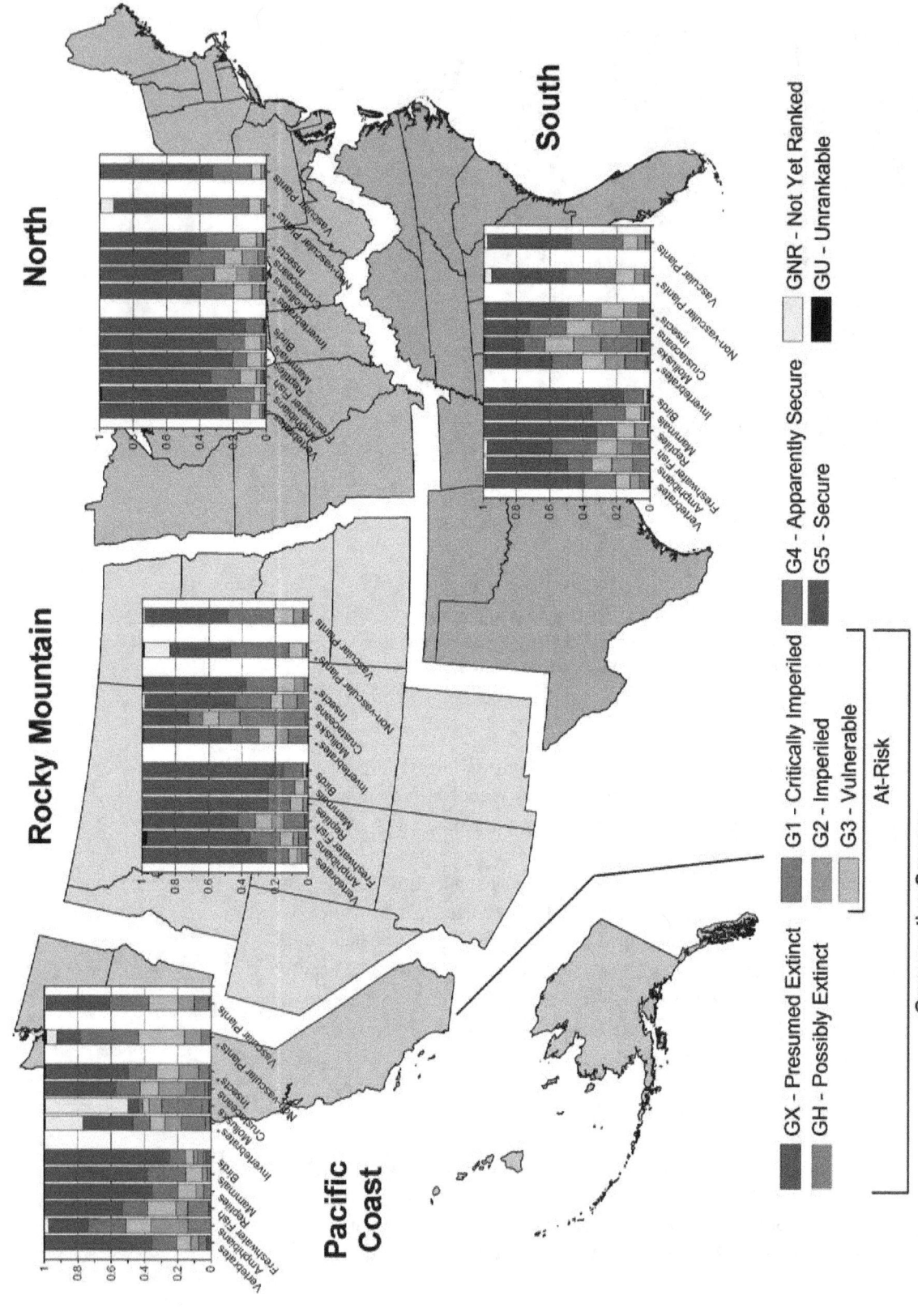

Figure 24—The proportion of species assigned to each NatureServe conservation status rank for vertebrates, invertebrates, and plants by RPA regions. Asterisks (*) indicate those taxonomic groups with uncertain proportions because many species are awaiting conservation assessments.

Geographic patterns of ESA listed and at-risk species occurrence

The geographic distribution of ESA-listed species has been shown to vary geographically (Flather and others 1994; Flather and others 1998), with prominent concentrations of threatened and endangered species occurring in Hawaii, the southern Appalachians, peninsular Florida, coastal areas, and the arid Southwest (Figure 25a). Generally, these areas of geographic concentration tend also to be consistent among major species groups although regional emphasis does vary among groups (Appendix C).

These patterns have remained largely unchanged for the past 15 years. Counties that have moved into the highest class of endangered species counts based on thresholds used in the 2000 RPA Assessment are often in proximity to counties that remained in the highest endangerment class for both the 2000 and 2010 RPA Assessments (Figure 25b). Exceptions to this pattern include emerging concentrations in the Midwest among scattered counties from east-central Missouri through northern Indiana; counties along portions of the Atlantic and Gulf coasts; eastern portions of the Edwards Plateau in Texas; the basin and range region of southern New Mexico; and the Colorado Plateau region of Utah.

The geographic concentrations of at-risk species based on NatureServe's criteria show decidedly more contiguous concentrations in peninsular Florida, the Florida panhandle, coastal California and Oregon, and the southwestern United States. (Figure 26a). These more contiguous concentrations of at-risk species show some degree of association with high human populations and their associated land use intensification (Florida and California), and areas known to support high numbers of species with restricted ranges (the arid southwest) (Stein and others 2000b).

The geographic pattern of extirpated species[8] tends to deviate significantly from the current distribution of listed or at-risk species—the exception being Hawaii (Figure 26b). Extirpated species are concentrated among Mid-Atlantic States—a pattern that indicates how much the historical biodiversity has been altered under human settlement. Given the higher proportion of public lands, the lower density of human populations (Mockrin and others 2012), and their larger size,[9] it is not surprising that western states have tended to lose fewer species than their eastern counterparts. The pattern of state-level extirpation noted here is consistent with patterns of population extirpation among species formally listed as threatened or endangered with Leidner and Neel (2011) noting that higher land conversion rates in the East were associated with greater levels of population extirpation than in the Interior West.

---

[8] Extirpation from a state is based on the state-level conservation ranks in NatureServe, which include species that historically occurred within a state but are now presumed (SX) or possibly (SH) extinct within that state. State extirpations often occur at the periphery of a species' geographic range.

[9] All other things being equal, small states are likely to have more extirpations because the range and abundance of species will be smaller than in large states.

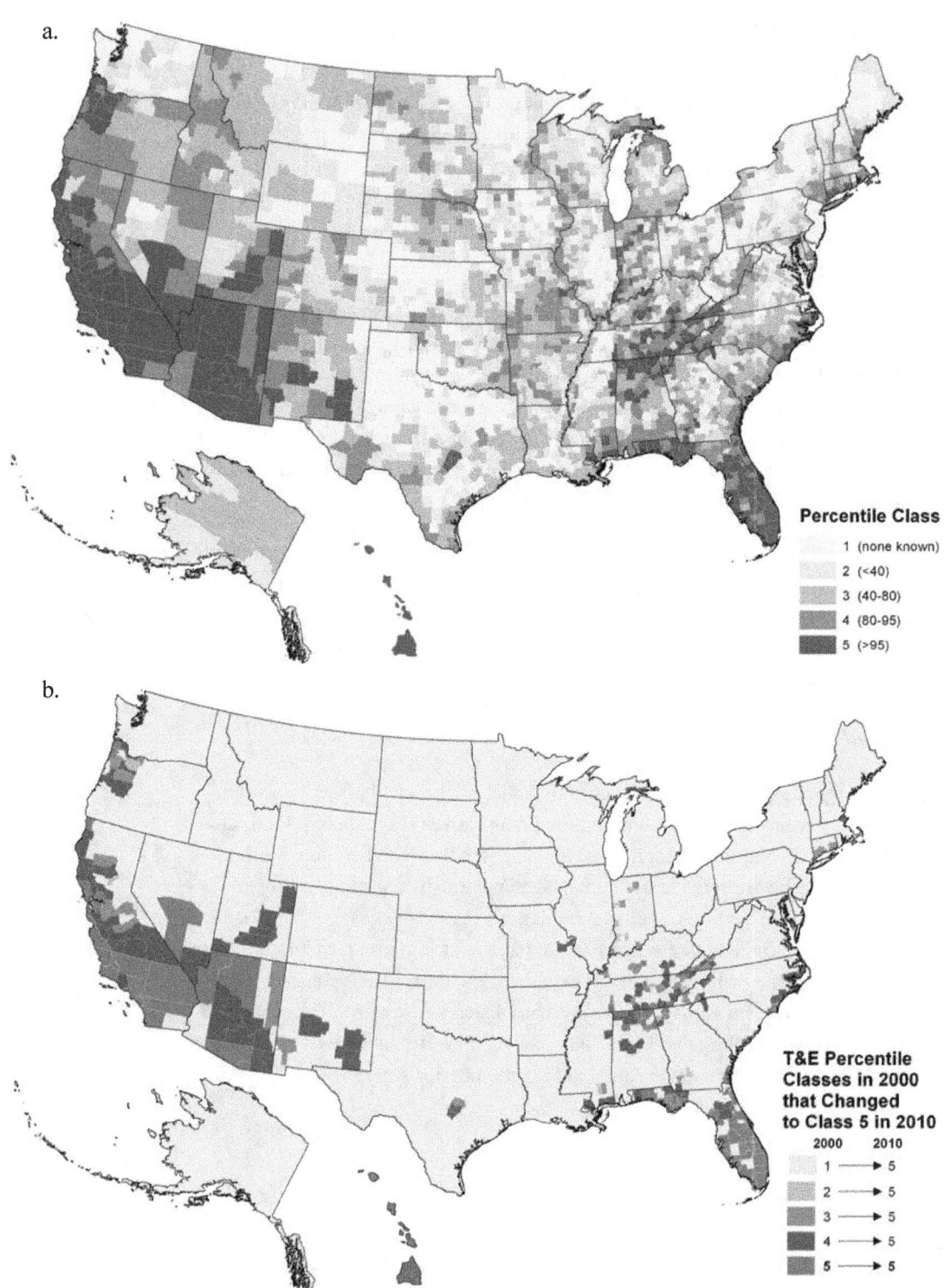

Figure 25—County-level counts of species formally listed as threatened or endangered in the United States (a). The legend categories (class 5 represents the highest counts of listed species) are based on percentile classes after ranking both large- and small-area counties (to account for differential county area as in the 2000 RPA Assessment). To display those counties that have increased numbers of listed species since the 2000 RPA Assessment, we show those counties (and their 2000 percentile class) that are now (2010 RPA Assessment) percentile class 5 (b). Those counties that were class 5 in the 2000 RPA Assessment and remained in class 5 for the 2010 RPA Assessment are shown in blue.

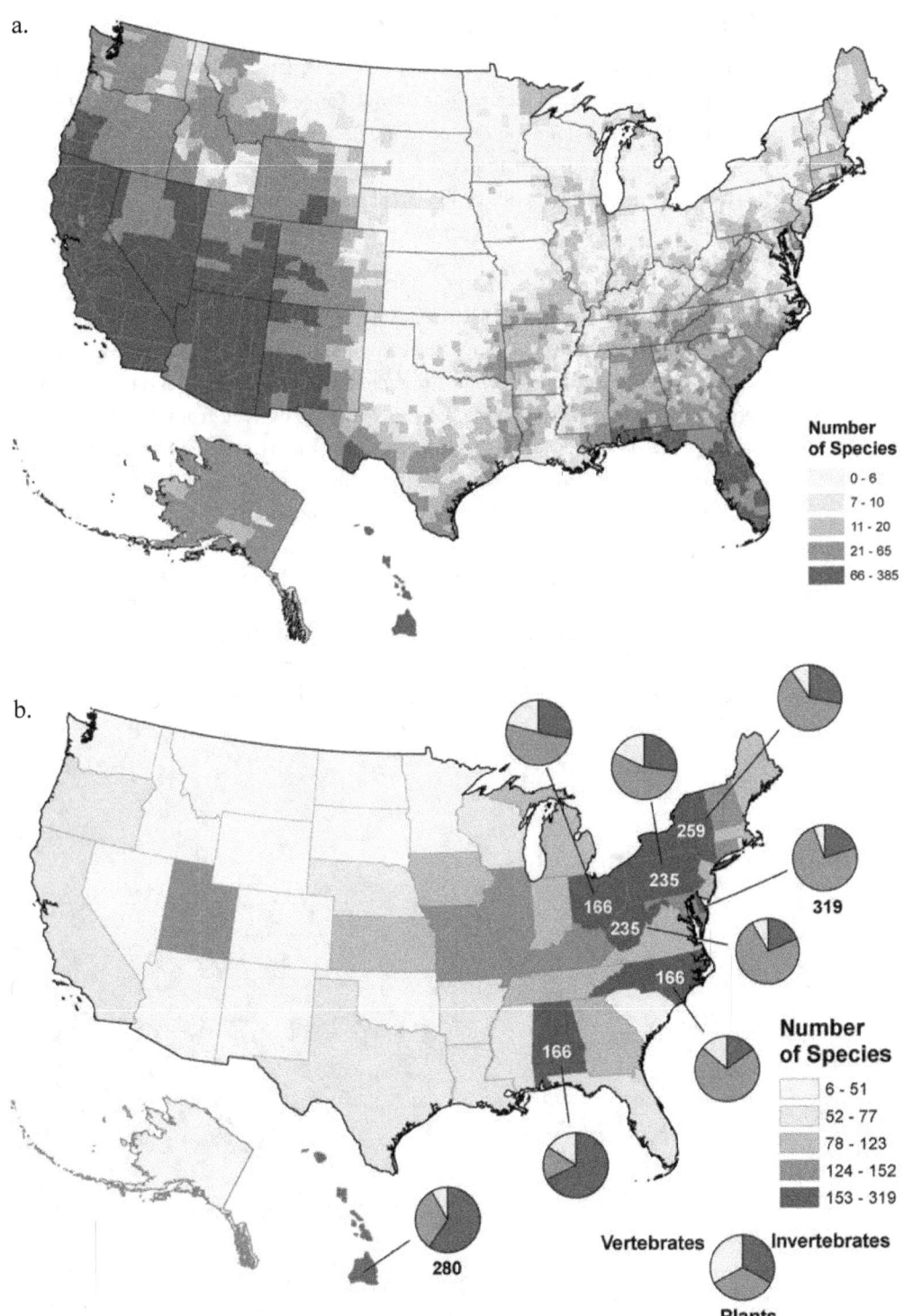

Figure 26—The geographic distribution of (a) county-level counts of species assessed to be at-risk of extinction (conservation status ranks G1, G2, and G3; legend categories reflect approximately the <40th percentile; 40-60th percentile; 60-80th percentile; 80-95th percentile; >95th percentile) and (b) state-level counts of species considered to be extirpated from a state (legend categories reflect approximately the <30th percentile; 30-50th percentile; 50-70th percentile; 70-85th percentile; >85th percentile; pie charts represent the proportion of extirpated species that were plant, vertebrate, and invertebrate species).

Projected Forest Bird Richness

Forest bird richness tends to be highest in areas characterized by greater topographic relief (Figure 27). Notable concentrations of high forest bird richness occur along the Appalachian Mountains, major mountain ranges of the Pacific Coast, the northern and central Rocky Mountains, and the Ozark and Ouachita highlands of Arkansas and Missouri. The mixed deciduous-coniferous forests of the Great Lakes region also support high numbers of forest breeding birds due to a high degree of habitat diversity associated with this boreal-hardwood transition.

Based on the statistical models as reported in Pidgeon and others (2007), we projected bird community response (change in the average number of forest bird species detected on a BBS route) to shifts in land use composition and housing density. Land use change projections provided by Wear (2011) and housing projections derived from the 2008 Woods and Poole county forecasts as described in Radeloff and others (2010) indicated that intensive land uses (urban and developed land) and housing density are expected to have an increased footprint on forested landscapes. By 2060, forest land is projected to decline across all three 2010 RPA scenarios by as much as 37.5 million acres under the assumptions characterizing scenario RPA A1B, to as little as 24.7 million acres under scenario RPA B2 (Wear 2011: Appendix C).

If we focus on the scenario indicative of the highest economic growth (RPA A1B), then forest bird communities are generally expected to support a lower variety of species (Figure 28) in response to projected changes in land use and housing. However, not all forest bird life-history groups were equally sensitive to the projected land uses and housing density. Those

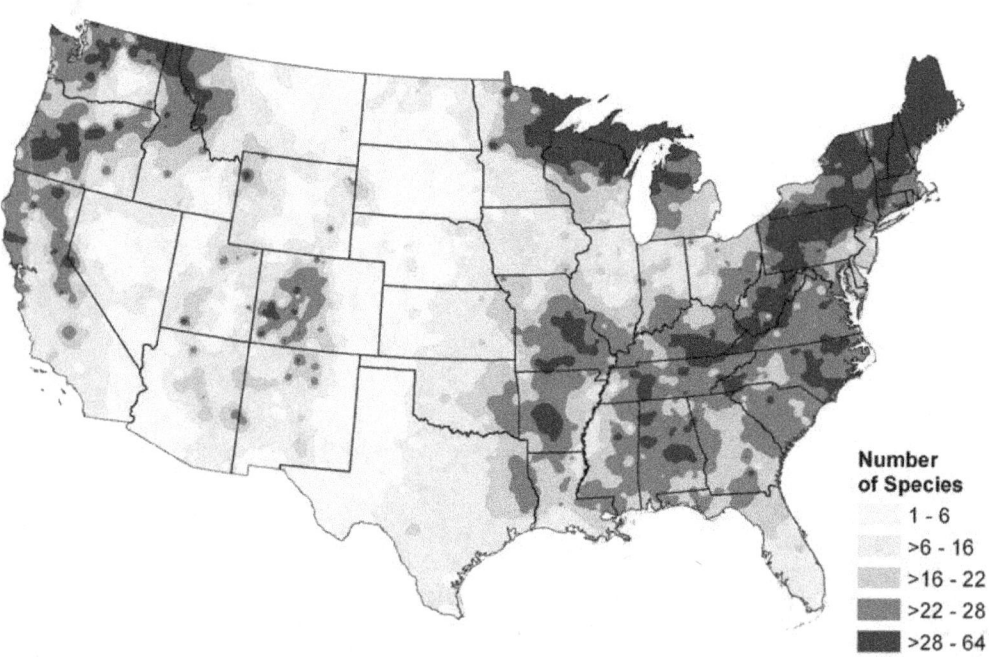

Number of Species

1 - 6
>6 - 16
>16 - 22
>22 - 28
>28 - 64

Figure 27—Mean estimated forest bird richness on a survey route over the 2007–2009 period using the North American Breeding Bird Survey.

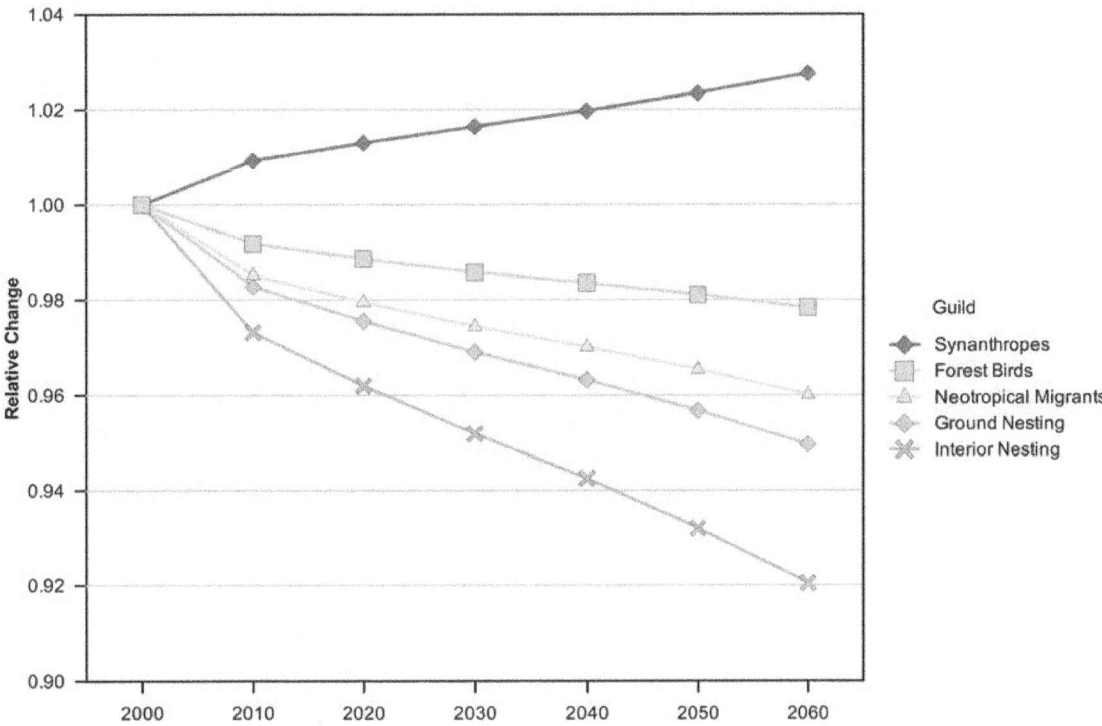

Figure 28—Projected changes in forest bird richness (by life-history group) based on land use and housing density changes projected to 2060 under scenario RPA A1B. See Table 4 for scenario characteristics.

species that prefer to nest in intact interior habitats (8 percent decline) or nest on or near the ground (5 percent decline) were the most sensitive bird groups to the projected land use and housing changes under scenario RPA A1B. The response of these species groups to increased land use intensification and home development is expected given their known sensitivities to habitat fragmentation and increased nest predation (Boulinier and others 2001; Donovan and Flather 2002; Vance and others 2003). Although we did not have a way of directly projecting patterns of forest habitat arrangement (for example, mean forest patch size, total forest edge, mean distance among forest patches), we know that measures of habitat arrangement correlate strongly with loss of the focal habitat type of interest (Flather and Bevers 2002). In the projections reviewed here, the loss of forest habitat would be certainly accompanied by an increase in forest fragmentation (see Riitters [2011] for review of landscape pattern metrics focused on forest habitats for the coterminous United States). The only bird group that showed a positive response (nearly a 3 percent gain) to the land use and housing projections under the RPA A1B scenario was that group referred to as synanthropic (Figure 28) —a collection of species that tolerate and thrive in habitats associated with human settlement.

Forest bird communities showed similar responses across the three alternative futures as specified in the scenarios examined (Figure 29a; see Table 4 for a description of the key characteristics of each RPA scenario). The least impact on forest bird richness was observed under scenario RPA B2—a future with lower population growth and intermediate economic growth

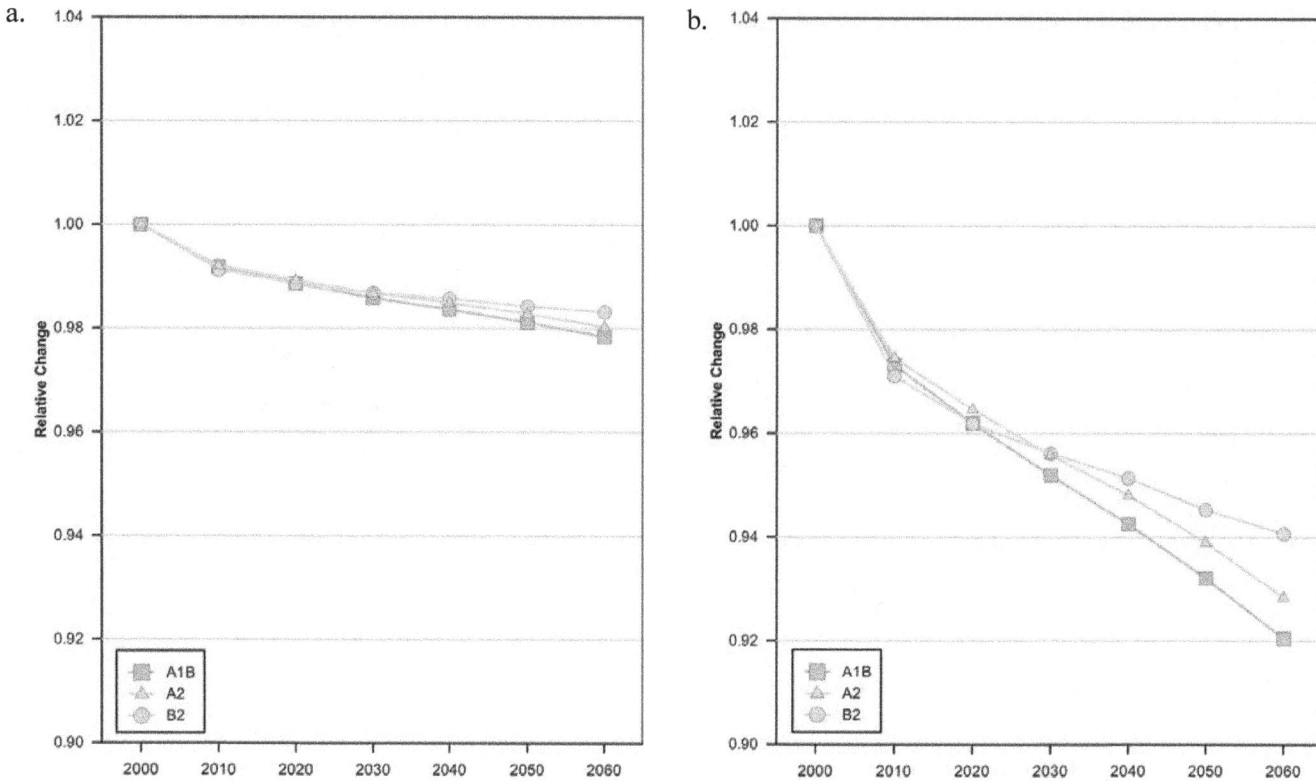

Figure 29—Changes in bird richness for each RPA scenario for (a) species that breed in forest habitats and (b) species that prefer to breed in interior forest conditions for each RPA scenario. See Table 4 for scenario characteristics.

where local solutions are favored over global integration. The greatest decline in forest richness was observed under scenario RPA A1B—a future characterized by more rapid economic growth. Forest birds that prefer to nest in interior habitats away from forest edges showed greater sensitivity among scenarios (Figure 29b). Again, the least impact was associated with scenario RPA B2 and the greatest impact was observed with RPA A1B. The difference between these two responses spanned only 2 percentage points, and even then such differences did not begin to manifest until 2040.

It should be emphasized that the forest bird community responses are driven by land development pressures on private lands. Conventional wisdom would suggest that bird communities occurring on public lands may be buffered from many of the pressures occurring on private lands that tend to reduce the variety of species that a particular landscape can support. Expanding human populations and attendant land use changes are the primary factors driving changes in biological diversity (Vitousek and others 1997), and forest habitats on private lands are being used more intensively by humans. Concurrent with this land use intensification, open lands are under increasing pressure from housing and road development to support an ever growing human population (http://www.fs.fed.us/openspace/). These development pressures are particularly strong on lands with high natural amenity values (Huston 2005)—lands which often occur in proximity to public lands in general and to national forests in particular (Radeloff and others 2010). As private lands bear the growing burden of human-associated ecosystem stresses, public lands are becoming increasingly important for the conservation of biological resources (Robles and others 2008; Flather and others 2009b). However, the ability of public lands to sustain important ecosystem services and biodiversity is affected by land use activities on the surrounding private lands.

In an effort to judge where human development pressures near public lands (including national forests, wilderness areas, and national parks) may put the conservation value of public lands most at risk, Radeloff and others (2010) examined housing development in and near public lands over a 60-year period. From 1940 to 2000, a total of 28 million homes were constructed within 30 miles of the protected areas examined in the study, with the majority of those homes (25.8 million) being built near national forests. Although wilderness areas receive the highest level of protection against development and resource extractions within their boundaries, they are not immune to development in the surrounding landscape—a total of 16.1 million new homes were built within 30 miles of wilderness area boundaries between 1940 and 2000. Areas within 30 miles of national parks saw the lowest gain in new housing unit construction (+1.5 million) over the 60-year period. An important issue to natural resource management is private inholdings within public lands. This phenomenon is particularly important for national forests because there can be substantial areas within the administrative boundary of a forest that remain in private ownership. Between 1940 and 2000 just over 940,000 new homes were constructed on these private inholdings—a gain that more than tripled housing density within this prized real estate.

The pattern of housing growth in the vicinity of protected lands also varied geographically. Because initial housing density in the 1940s was relatively low, the relative rate of housing growth by the year 2000 has been the greatest in the West (Figure 30a). Eastern protected areas show relatively lower relative growth rates but have witnessed the greatest absolute gain in new home construction (Figure 30b). Of particular note are those areas of the country where relative and absolute housing growth have both been high. Areas qualifying in this regard include peninsular Florida; the southern Appalachians; the foothill and front ranges near major metropolitan areas in Colorado, Utah, and Washington; montane habitats in the arid Southwest; and southern California—many of the same geographic areas that also support particularly high concentrations of imperiled species (see Figures 25 and 26).

The establishment of protected areas, whether they are focused on biodiversity conservation or allow for some degree of multiple-use management, is an important conservation strategy that has long been thought to offer sanctuary from human activities (Flather and others 2009b). However, growing human populations are extending the human footprint and are projected to have broad global impacts on biodiversity conservation (Sala and others 2000). Because public lands attract development, the potential ecological consequences of housing growth could be substantial and a particularly difficult management issue to address given that public land stewards in general, and the Forest Service in particular, have a limited portfolio of conservation strategies that can affect land use patterns on private lands.

a.

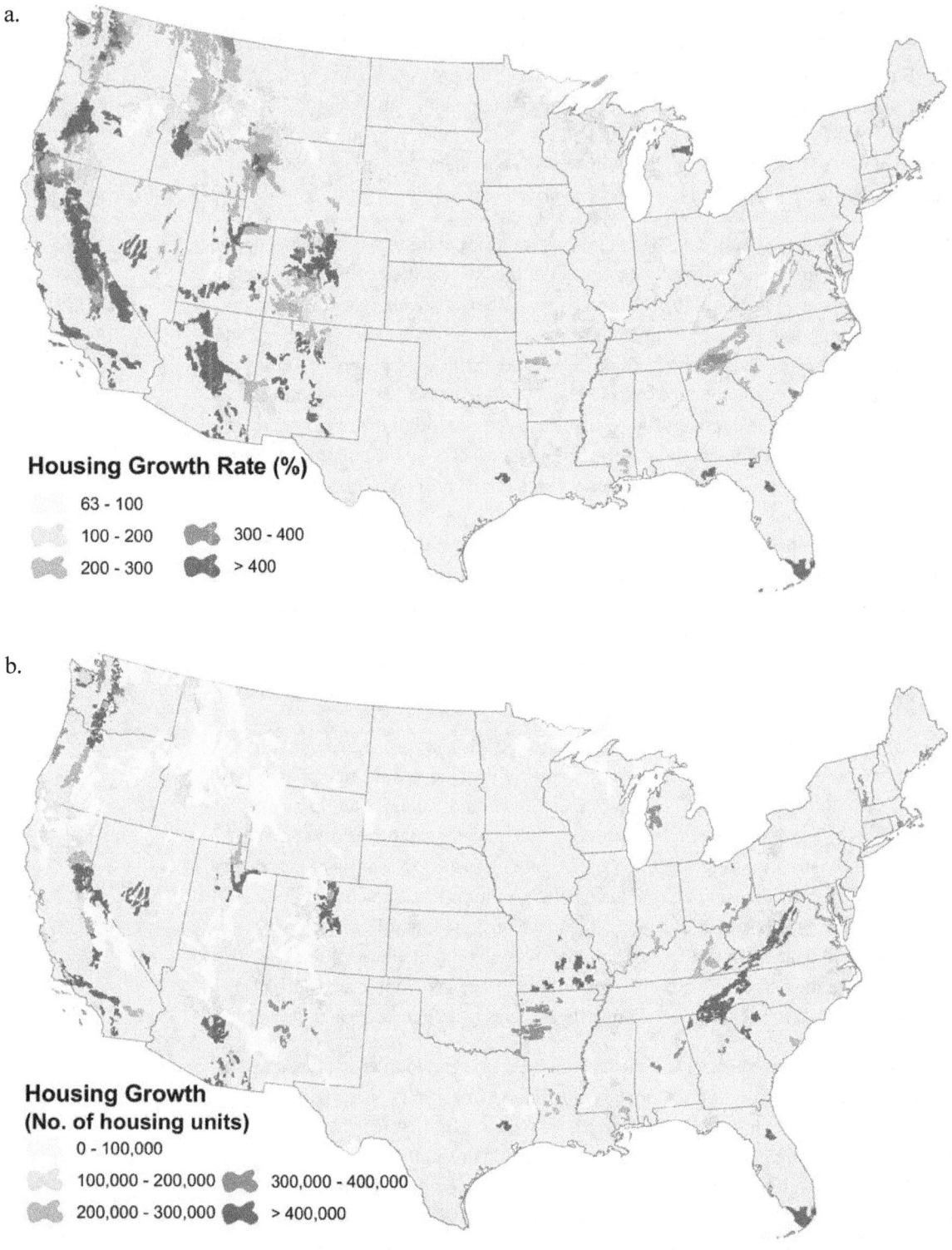

Housing Growth Rate (%)

63 - 100

100 - 200   300 - 400

200 - 300   > 400

b.

**Housing Growth
(No. of housing units)**

0 - 100,000

100,000 - 200,000   300,000 - 400,000

200,000 - 300,000   > 400,000

Figure 30—Housing growth rates observed within a 30-mile buffer around the outer boundary of each national forest, wilderness area, and national park over the period 1940–2000. Both (a) relative and (b) absolute housing growth rates are depicted.

Conclusions

The historical trends in wildlife populations and harvests have varied depending on the species or species group considered. This variation in historical trajectories is no doubt caused by a complex interaction involving:

- land use changes that can convert or create habitats for different sets of species;

- shifts in the intensity with which humans manage lands that can differentially affect species habitat;

- shifts in public demands and preferences for goods and services provided by wildlife;

- and interactions among wildlife species themselves.

Because wildlife resources are so diverse, it is difficult, if not untenable, to offer a general statement of resource status. For that reason we will highlight resource trends by the broad species groups that served as the organizing framework for this report.

Summary of the 2010 RPA Assessment Findings

A general pattern of increasing population and harvest trends was observed among big game and waterfowl species. When considered in a historical context, the observed trends in these two groups of species are often considered wildlife management success stories (Organ and others 2010). Given that participation among persons who pursue big game and migratory game birds recreationally is steady or declining slightly (see Mockrin and others 2012), the population trends reviewed here suggest that supplies of animals to harvest are sufficient to meet the demands of recreational hunters. However, population gains are not immune to negative resource consequences. Habitats have limits on their capacity to sustainably support individuals, and there is evidence that some species may be exceeding those limits. White-tailed deer and several species of geese are commonly referred to as "overabundant," and these population excesses are being blamed for widespread habitat degradation (Ankney 1996; Côté and others 2004; Hurley and others 2012; Newson and others 2012). Because there remains a strong interest in maintaining harvestable numbers of these species, efforts to reduce populations are often met with public resistance. Therefore, the long-term population increases observed among these species represent an emerging unfavorable and controversial resource management topic that is deserving of closer scientific and management scrutiny from the ecological, biological, and social perspectives (Menu and others 2002; Levy 2006; Alisauskas and others 2011).

For many small game species and webless migratory game birds, population and harvest trends deviate notably from the trends observed among big game and waterfowl. Webless migratory game birds show general population and harvest declines, and the declines have been substantive for woodcock. Resident small game trends are more difficult to assess given the limited population monitoring data available from state wildlife agencies. Harvest trends have declined among many species, although much of this harvest reduction is likely attributable to declining participation in small game hunting (see Mockrin and others 2012) rather than a general indication of deteriorating populations. However, population trends among upland game birds derived from the BBS (in particular, northern bobwhite, scaled quail, sage grouse) suggest that small game harvest declines may have a component that is attributable to population reductions among some of these species. Small game species, particularly those associated with grassland, farmland, and early successional habitats, show very little sign of recovery from the declines noted in the 1989 and 2000 RPA Assessments (Flather and Hoekstra 1989; Flather and others 1999). Although there is local evidence that small game species can respond favorably to geographically extensive land use policies that provide suitable habitat (Brennan and Kuvlesky 2005), these local benefits have not yet manifested into population and harvest benefits at regional and national scales. For this reason, the trends in these species remain an important and unsolved management issue of concern.

Furbearers are a special case because the data we reviewed focuses solely on harvest. Fur harvests can change for a number of reasons that are independent of population levels, including changes in pelt prices, the number of trappers and their effort in pursuing furbearers, and changes in the accessibility of land for trapping. Moreover, there are some segments of society that are engaged in efforts to reduce this activity. The sum of these factors has resulted in notable fur harvest declines since the 2000 RPA Assessment, and wildlife damage complaints associated with furbearers are likely to become a more prominent management issue in the absence of any economic incentives to increase harvests.

For the most diverse species group covered in this assessment—nongame species that are not consumptively taken for sport, subsistence, or profit—we lack comprehensive monitoring systems for most species. A notable exception is for birds breeding in the United States. For the 426 species with sufficient data to estimate nationwide trends, 45 percent had stable abundance since the mid-1960s. A higher percentage of species had declining trends (31 percent) than increasing trends (24 percent) during the 1966 – 2008 period. Species groups that nest on or near the ground or in grassland habitats had relatively high proportions of species with declining trends. RPA regions already characterized by prominent human effects (the North and South regions) tended to have higher proportions of species with declining abundance. Cavity nesting species, permanent residents, and species preferring to breed in wetland habitats had a greater percentage of species with increasing trends than decreasing trends. There is also evidence that bird populations have fared better since the 2000 RPA Assessment with a greater proportion of species showing increasing trends. However, given the human population, land use, and housing development projections across the three 2010 RPA scenarios that define a set of alternative futures, it seems unlikely that bird populations will continue to improve in the future. As human populations grow, native habitats are lost to road construction, urbanization, and low density housing development. The 2010 RPA land use projections indicate that intensive land uses and housing development are expected to increase in forested landscapes. In response to these land use changes, most forest bird communities are expected to support a lower variety of species, particularly among those forest species that prefer intact interior habitats (that is, low fragmentation) or nest on or near the ground. The only group of birds expected to show an increase in species richness are those associated with human settlements. These patterns of bird richness response were similar across all RPA scenarios.

The trends in species of conservation concern reviewed in this assessment indicated that biodiversity writ large in the United States has continued to erode. Since the 2000 RPA

Assessment, there has been a net gain of 278 species formally listed as threatened or endangered under the ESA. The greatest gains were among plants (152 species), fish (31 species), insects (27 species), mollusks (20 species), and amphibians (8 species). Formally listed species tend to be concentrated in Hawaii, the southern Appalachians, peninsular Florida, coastal areas, and the arid Southwest. This pattern remained generally consistent with the 2000 RPA Assessment, although the geographic footprint of the areas supporting high counts of listed species has expanded. A focus on where species of conservation concern currently occur overlooks places where they have become extirpated. The number of species extirpated from each State showed areas of concentration in Hawaii and among the heavily populated Mid-Atlantic States—a pattern that indicates how much of the historical biodiversity has been altered under human settlement. These national patterns parallel what has been observed globally (see Mooney and Mace 2009; Stokstad 2010)—namely biodiversity continues to decline despite a growing trend in conservation investment (Rands and others 2010; Shifley, in press).

Resource Challenges and Future Opportunities

The 2010 RPA Assessment findings indicate that America's wildlife resources will continue to be pressured by the diverse and oftentimes competing demands for goods and services that are derived from a finite land base. Growing human populations coupled with economic growth will alter habitats that will, in turn, affect the composition and abundance of species that can be supported on managed landscapes. This rich and complex interaction between ecosystems and the human manipulation of those systems to meet societal demands for natural resource products provides the backdrop against which notable resource management challenges and opportunities can be identified and addressed.

Broadening the wildlife resource monitoring base

Resource monitoring systems that lead to unbiased and precise estimates of population size and harvest are fundamental to effective management of wildlife resources (Williams and others 2002). This wildlife assessment has relied on existing monitoring data from numerous sources (see Table 1). Despite these numerous sources, the availability of quantitative monitoring to support geographically and temporally extensive evaluations of wildlife status and trends has been, and continues to be, limited. Even among well-studied species, most lack standardized, statistically designed inventories to support broad-scale evaluations of status and trend in populations or harvests over the geographic and temporal scales that will be necessary to evaluate whether they are being managed sustainably (National Research Council 1992; Flather and others 2004). Certainly there are exceptions to this general claim of limited broad-scale monitoring data; notable examples with long-term data include the North American waterfowl monitoring system (Nichols and others 1995) and the North American Breeding Bird Survey (Robbins and others 1986). Moreover, recent efforts to extend BBS-type survey design to amphibians (see the North American Amphibian Monitoring Program; http://www.pwrc.usgs.gov/naamp/) have made substantial progress establishing a sampling design and a set of unified protocols (Weir and Mossman 2005) that will provide data that supports trend analyses across broad geographic areas. These data have supported state (Weir and others 2005) and regional (Weir and others 2009) occupancy trend analyses and—with further refinements to the protocol (Weir and Mossman 2005) and a longer record of observations—will provide a much needed database with which to assess amphibian status and trends.

These successes notwithstanding, there is a critical need to develop surveys that can quantify species distribution and abundance patterns for a much broader set of taxa (National Research Council 1992). The situation among resident mammals and birds that are sought by recreational hunters is further complicated by the fact that state jurisdiction over their management can lead to difficulty when merging inventory data across state boundaries. These difficulties notwithstanding, improvements to monitoring protocols and data-merging to address multi-jurisdictional and regional resource issues are needed if resource planners and managers are to allocate harvest or restore habitats efficiently (Mason and others 2006).

Geographic variation in wildlife resources will require regional and local strategies

Perhaps one of the most general conclusions that can be drawn from the 2010 RPA Assessment effort, regardless of the resource area of focus, is that drivers of resource change and resource responses vary from place to place. Threatened and endangered species cluster in certain geographic regions; bird species in one part of their range are increasing in response to habitat changes while in another part of their range their numbers are declining; game harvests in some management units have been increasing while in others they are declining; all are examples of statements about wildlife resource status and trends that appear throughout this document. Such an observation is not surprising. The United States has an abundance of wildlife resources, and that abundance varies as a function of the inherent productivity of ecosystems and the intensity with which humans use those ecosystems to grow crops, build infrastructure, or recreate on the landscape. Given this geographic variation in inherent ecosystem productivity and human impacts, it will be important to develop policies and management strategies that are flexible enough to be effective under a wide range of conditions and to acknowledge that the portfolio of conservation instruments (purchase/easements, habitat retention incentives, active restoration) will also have to vary among the diverse ecosystems supporting wildlife resources.

Integrated management to conserve biodiversity

Conservation science is concerned with anticipating how human-induced disturbance to ecosystems will affect the pattern of commonness and rarity of the biota inhabiting that system (Flather and Sieg 2007). In a world with limited resources to direct toward biodiversity conservation, a common priority-setting strategy has been to focus on that subset of species that is thought to have the highest extinction risk (Flather and others 1998; Flather and others 2011). Targeting species that are vulnerable to extinction has become especially important because recent estimates of global extinction rates are 2-3 orders of magnitude greater than the so-called natural background level (Levin and Levin 2002). Because important ecosystem functions can be degraded by the loss of species, there is concern that the goods and services humans derive from ecological systems will become diminished as more species are lost or threatened with extinction.

Fortunately, the United States is characterized by substantial public lands that are critically important to sustaining extant populations of species of conservation concern (Flather and others 1994). Lands under the resource stewardship responsibility of the U.S. Forest Service have been shown recently to provide habitat for more listed and imperiled species than under any other federal agency (Stein and others 2008). Given the increasing land use pressures on private lands and the growing demands for living in high-amenity areas adjacent to national forests (Radeloff and others 2010), public lands like national forests and grasslands will serve a growing role in the conservation of imperiled species. However, conserving biodiversity will be unsuccessful if restricted to public land management. In an analysis focused on forest species of conservation concern (6,187 species), Robles and others (2008) found that 60 percent of these species occurred on private forests in the coterminous United States. Unfortunately, many areas, particularly in the southeastern United States, that support concentrations of at-risk species on private lands are also considered to have a high risk of forest conversion by 2030 (Robles and others 2008; Stein and others 2010).

Collaborative efforts that span public and private land ownerships, and span all three Forest Service Programs (Research and Development, National Forest System, and State and Private Forestry), will be vital to maintaining the nation's flora and fauna. Failure to take a broad programmatic and policy view of biodiversity conservation will further risk the erosion of our biological heritage. Designing monitoring strategies, discovering habitat relationships, and completing population viability assessments will require increasing research investments to document population trends, identify emerging at-risk species, design management to recover at-risk species, and determine when key populations have been restored—all of which increase our conservation capacity. The National Forest System and State and Private Forestry programs will need to implement complementary actions to preserve and restore habitats through (1) land acquisition or conservation easements that will target priority areas via public-private partnerships, (2) design of cost-reduction and tax incentive programs that facilitate species conservation (e.g., USDA's Forest Legacy and Forest Stewardship Programs), (3) development of resource certification systems that require biodiversity conservation standards (Robles and others 2008), and (4) development of market-based instruments to reward landowners for biodiversity conservation (Jenkins and others 2004; Goldstein and others 2006; Pascual and Perrings 2007).

References

Adams, M. J.; Muths, E.; Grant, E. H. C.; Miller, D. A.; Waddle, J. H.; Walls, S. C., et al. 2012. The U.S. Geological Survey Amphibian Research and Monitoring Initiative – 2011 annual update Fact Sheet 2012-3090. U.S. Department of the Interior, U.S. Geological Survey. 4 p. (available online: http://pubs.usgs.gov/fs/2012/3090/).

Afton, A. D.; Anderson, M. G. 2001. Declining scaup populations: a retrospective analysis of long-term population and harvest survey data. Journal of Wildlife Management 65: 781-796.

Aldridge, C. L.; Nielsen, S. E.; Beyer, H. L.; Boyce, M. S.; Connelly, J. W.; Knick, S. T., et al. 2008. Range-wide patterns of greater sage-grouse persistence. Diversity and Distributions 14: 983-994.

Alford, R. A. 2011. Bleak future for amphibian. Nature 480: 461-462.

Alisauskas, R. T.; Rockwell, R. F.; Dufour, K. W.; Cooch, E. G.; Zimmerman, G.; Drake, K. L., et al. 2011. Harvest, survival, and abundance of midcontinent lesser snow geese relative to population reduction efforts. Wildlife Monographs 179: 1-42.

Andelt, W. F.; Phillips, R. L.; Schmidt, R. H.; Gill, R. B. 1999. Trapping furbearers: an overview of the biological and social issues surrounding a public policy controversy. Wildlife Society Bulletin 27: 53-64.

Ankney, C. D. 1996. An embarrassment of riches: too many geese. Journal of Wildlife Management 60: 217-223.

Association of Fish and Wildlife Agencies. 2010. U.S. furharvest estimates. Washington, DC: Association of Fish and Wildlife Agencies (available online: http://jjcdev.com/~fishwild/?section=furbearer_management_resources).

Bailey, R. G. 1995. Description of the ecoregions of the United States. Second edition revised and expanded. Miscellaneous Publication Number 1391. Washington, DC: USDA, Forest Service.

Balmfort, A.; Bond, W. 2005. Trends in the state of nature and their implications for human well-being. Ecology Letters 8: 1218-1234.

Beebee, T. J. C.; Griffiths, R. A. 2005. The amphibian decline crisis: a watershed for conservation biology? Biological Conservation 125: 271-285.

Benjamini, Y.; Hochberg, Y. 1995. Controlling the false discovery rate - a practical and powerful approach to multiple testing. Journal of the Royal Statistical Society Series B-Methodological 57: 289-300.

Berlanga, H.; Kennedy, J. A.; Rich, T. D.; Arizmendi, M. C.; Beardmore, C. J.; Blancher, P. J., et al. 2010. Saving our shared birds: Partners in Flight Tri-National vision for landbird conservation. Ithaca, NY: Cornell Lab of Ornithology. 49 p.

Blaustein, A. R. 1994. Chicken little or Nero's fiddle? A perspective on declining amphibian populations. Herpetologica 50: 85-97.

Blaustein, A. R.; Hoffman, P. D.; Hokit, D. G.; Kiesecker, J. M.; Walls, S. C.; Hays, J. B. 1994a. UV repair and resistance to solar UV-B in amphibian eggs – a link to population declines. Proceedings of the National Academy of Sciences, USA 91: 1791-1795.

Blaustein, A. R.; Hokit, D. G.; Ohara, R. K.; Holt, R. A. 1994b. Pathogenic fungus contributes to amphibian losses in the Pacific-Northwest. Biological Conservation 67: 251-254.

Blaustein, A. R.; Wake, D. B. 1990. Declining amphibian populations – a global phenomenon. Trends in Ecology & Evolution 5: 203-204.

Blehert, D. S.; Hicks, A. C.; Behr, M.; Meteyer, C. U.; Berlowski-Zier, B. M.; Buckles, E. L., et al. 2009. Bat white-nose syndrome: an emerging fungal pathogen? Science 323: 227.

Boulinier, T.; Nichols, J. D.; Hines, J. E.; Sauer, J. R.; Flather, C. H.; Pollock, K. H. 2001. Forest fragmentation and bird community dynamics: Inference at regional scales. Ecology 82: 1159-1169.

Boyles, J. G.; Cryan, P. M.; McCracken, G. F.; Kunz, T. H. 2011. Economic importance of bats in agriculture. Science 332: 41-42.

Bradford, D. F. 2005. Factors implicated in amphibian population declines in the United States. In: Lannoo, M., ed. Amphibian declines: the conservation status of United States species. Berkeley, CA: University of California Press: 915-925.

Brennan, L. A.; Kuvlesky, W. P. 2005. North American grassland birds: an unfolding conservation crisis? Journal of Wildlife Management 69: 1-13.

Brennan, L.; DeMaso, S.; Guthery, F.; Hardin, J.; Kowaleski, C.; Lerich, S., et al. 2005. Where have all the quail gone? Texas Quail Initiative. 21 p.

Brosi, B. J.; Biber, E. G. N. 2012. Citizen involvement in the US Endangered Species Act. Science 337: 802-803.

Butchart, S. H. M.; Baillie, J. E. M.; Chenery, A. M.; Collen, B.; Gregory, R. D.; Revenga, C., et al. 2010. National indicators show biodiversity progress response. Science 329: 900-901.

Cameron, S. A.; Lozier, J. D.; Strange, J. P.; Koch, J. B.; Cordes, N.; Solter, L. F., et al. 2011. Patterns of widespread decline in North American bumble bees. Proceedings of the National Academy of Sciences, USA 108: 662-667.

Cardinale, B. J.; Srivastava, D. S.; Duffy, J. E.; Wright, J. P.; Downing, A. L.; Sankaran, M., et al. 2006. Effects of biodiversity on the functioning of trophic groups and ecosystems. Nature 443: 989-992.

Chandler, W. J. 1985. Migratory bird protection and management. In: Di Silvestro, R. L., ed. Audubon wildlife report 1985. New York: The National Audubon Society: 27-70.

Chapin, F. S.; Zavaleta, E. S.; Eviner, V. T.; Naylor, R. L.; Vitousek, P. M.; Reynolds, H. L., et al. 2000. Consequences of changing biodiversity. Nature 405: 234-242.

Conover, M. R. 2001. Effect of hunting and trapping on wildlife damage. Wildlife Society Bulletin 29: 521-532.

Cooper, T. R.; Parker, K. 2009. American woodcock population status, 2009. Laurel, MD: U.S. Department of the Interior, Fish and Wildlife Service. 15 p.

Cooper, T. R.; Parker, K. 2010. American woodcock population status, 2010. Laurel, MD: U.S. Department of the Interior, Fish and Wildlife Service. 16 p.

Cooper, T. R.; Parker, K.; Rau, R. D. 2008. American woodcock population status, 2008. Laurel, MD: U.S. Department of the Interior, Fish and Wildlife Service. 15 p.

Copeland, H. E.; Doherty, K. E.; Naugle, D. E.; Pocewicz, A.; Kiesecker, J. M. 2009. Mapping oil and gas development potential in the US intermountain west and estimating impacts to species. Public Library of Science ONE 4(10).

Cortner, H. J.; Schwitzer, D. L. 1981. Institutional limits to national public planning for forest resources: the Resources Planning Act. Natural Resources Journal 21: 203-222.

Côté, S. D.; Rooney, T. P.; Tremblay, J. P.; Dussault, C.; Waller, D. M. 2004. Ecological impacts of deer overabundance. Annual Review of Ecology Evolution and Systematics 35: 113-147.

Cryan, P. M.; Meteyer, C. U.; Boyles, J. G.; Blehert, D. S. 2010. Wing pathology of white-nose syndrome in bats suggests life-threatening disruption of physiology. BioMed Central Biology 8:135.

Daily, G. C. 1997. Nature's services: societal dependence on natural ecosystems. Washington, DC: Island Press. 392 p.

Dessecker, D. R.; McAuley, D. G. 2001. Importance of early successional habitat to ruffed grouse and American woodcock. Wildlife Society Bulletin 29: 456-465.

DeVink, J. M.; Berezanski, D.; Imrie, D. 2011. Comments on Brodie and Post: harvest effort: the missing covariate in analyses of furbearer harvest data. Population Ecology 53: 261-262.

Donovan, T. M.; Flather, C. H. 2002. Relationships among North American songbird trends, habitat fragmentation, and landscape occupancy. Ecological Applications 12: 364-374.

Drever, M. C.; Martin, K. 2010. Response of woodpeckers to changes in forest health and harvest: Implications for conservation of avian biodiversity. Forest Ecology and Management 259: 958-966.

Droege, S. 1990. The North American Breeding Bird Survey. In: Sauer, J.R.; Droege, S., eds. Survey designs and statistical methods for estimation of avian population trends. Biological Report 90. Washington, DC: U.S. Department of the Interior, U.S. Fish and Wildlife Service. 1-4.

Duda, M. D.; Jones, M. F.; Criscione, A. 2010. The sportman's voice: hunting and fishing in America. State College, PA: Venture Publishing. 259 p.

Dunson, W. A.; Wyman, R. L.; Corbett, E. S. 1992. A symposium on amphibian declines and habitat acidification. Journal of Herpetology 26: 349-352.

Ehrlich, P. R.; Pringle, R. M. 2008. Where does biodiversity go from here? A grim buisness-as-usual forecast and a hopeful portfolio of partial solutions. Proceedings of the National Academy of Sciences, USA 105: 11579-11586.

Ellison, L. E.; O'Shea, T. J.; Bogan, M. A.; Everette, A. L.; Schneider, D. M. 2003. Existing data on colonies of bats in the United States: summary and analysis of the U.S. Geological Survey's Bat Population Database. In: O'Shea, T.J.; Bogan, M. A., eds. Monitoring trends in bat populations of the United States and territories: problems and prospects. Information and Technology Report 2003–0003. U.S. Department of the Interior, U.S. Geological Survey. 127-237.

Fisher, B.; Turner, R. K.; Morling, P. 2009. Defining and classifying ecosystem services for decision making. Ecological Economics 68: 643-653.

Fisher, R. N.; Shaffer, H. B. 1996. The decline of amphibians in California's Great Central Valley. Conservation Biology 10: 1387-1397.

Flather, C. H. 1996. Fitting species-accumulation functions and assessing regional land use impacts on avian diversity. Journal of Biogeography 23: 155-168.

Flather, C. H.; Bevers, M. 2002. Patchy reaction-diffusion and population abundance: The relative importance of habitat amount and arrangement. American Naturalist 159: 40-56.

Flather, C. H.; Brady, S. J.; Knowles, M. S. 1999. Wildlife resource trends in the United States: a technical document supporting the 2000 USDA Forest Service RPA Assessment. Gen. Tech. Rep. RMRS-GTR-33. Fort Collins, CO: U.S. Department of Agriculture, Rocky Mountain Research Station. 79 p.

Flather, C. H.; Hayward, G. D.; Beissinger, S. R.; Stephens, P. A. 2011. Minimum viable populations: is there a "magic number" for conservation practitioners? Trends in Ecology & Evolution 26: 307-316.

Flather, C. H.; Hoekstra, T. W. 1989. An analysis of the wildlife and fish situation in the United States: 1989-2040. Gen. Tech. Rep. RM-78. Fort Collins, CO: U.S. Department of Agriculture, Forest Service, Rocky Mountain Research Station. 146 p.

Flather, C. H.; Joyce, L. A.; Bloomgarden, C. A. 1994. Species endangerment patterns in the United States. Gen. Tech. Rep. RM-241. Fort Collins, CO: U.S. Department of Agriculture, Forest Service, Rocky Mountain Research Station. 42 p.

Flather, C. H.; Knowles, M. S.; Kendall, I. A. 1998. Threatened and endangered species geography. BioScience 48: 365-376.

Flather, C. H.; Knowles, M. S.; McNees, J. 2008. Geographic patterns of at-risk species. Gen. Tech. Rep. RMRS-GTR-211. Fort Collins, CO: U.S. Department of Agriculture, Forest Service, Rocky Mountain Research Station. 21 p.

Flather, C. H.; Knowles, M. S.; Brady, S. J. 2009a. Population and harvest trends of big game and small game species: a technical document supporting the USDA Forest Service Interim Update of the 2000 RPA Assessment. Gen. Tech. Rep. RMRS-GTR-219. Fort Collins, CO: U.S. Department of Agriculture, Forest Service, Rocky Mountain Research Station. 34 p.

Flather, C. H.; Knowles, M. S.; McNees, J. In press. Criterion 1: Conservation biological diversity. Indicator 5: Number and status of native forest associated species at risk, as determined by legislation or scientific assessment. In: Data report: a supplement to the national report on sustainable forests–2010. FS-000. Washington, DC: U.S. Department of Agriculture, Forest Service.

Flather, C. H.; Ricketts, T. H.; Sieg, C. H.; Knowles, M. S.; Fay, J. P.; McNees, J. 2004. Criterion 1: Conservation of biological diversity. Indicator 6: The number of forest dependent species. In: D. Darr, coord. Data report: a supplement to the national report on sustainable forests–2003. FS-766A. Washington, DC: U.S. Department of Agriculture, Forest Service.

Flather, C. H.; Sauer, J. R. 1996. Using landscape ecology to test hypotheses about large-scale abundance patterns in migratory birds. Ecology 77: 28-35.

Flather, C. H.; Sieg, C. H. 2000. Applicability of Montreal Process Criterion 1 – conservation of biological diversity – to rangeland sustainability. International Journal of Sustainable Development and World Ecology 7: 81-96.

Flather, C. H.; Sieg, C. H. 2007. Species rarity: definition, causes, and classification. In: Raphael, M. G.; Molina, R., eds. Conservation of rare or little-known species. Washington, DC: Island Press: 40-66.

Flather, C. H.; Wilson, K. R.; Shriner, S. A. 2009b. Geographic approaches to biodiversity conservation: implications of scale and error to landscape planning. In: Millspaugh, Joshua J.; Thompson, Frank R., eds. Models for planning wildlife conservation in large landscapes. Burlington, MA: Academic Press: 85-122.

Foden, W. B.; Mace, G. M.; Vié, J.-C.; Angulo, A.; Butchart, S. H. M.; DeVantier, L., et al. 2009. Species susceptibility to climate change impacts. In: Vié, J.-C.; Hilton-Taylor, C.; Stuart, S. N., eds. Wildlife in a changing world: an analysis of the 2008 IUCN Red List of threatened species. Gland, CH: IUCN: 77-87.

Frick, W. F.; Pollock, J. F.; Hicks, A. C.; Langwig, K. E.; Reynolds, D. S.; Turner, G. G., et al. 2010. An emerging disease causes regional population collapse of a common North American bat species. Science 329: 679-682.

Gargas, A.; Trest, M. T.; Christensen, M.; Volk, T. J.; Blehert, D. S. 2009. *Geomyces destructans* sp. nov. associated with bat white-nose syndrome. Mycotaxon 108: 147-154.

Ghazoul, J. 2005a. Buzziness as usual? Questioning the global pollination crisis. Trends in Ecology & Evolution 20: 367-373.

Ghazoul, J. 2005b. Response to Steffan-Dewenter et al.: questioning the global pollination crisis. Trends in Ecology & Evolution 20: 652-653.

Goldstein, J. H.; Daily, G. C.; Friday, J. B.; Matson, P. A.; Naylor, R. A. 2006. Business strategies for conservation on private lands: Koa forestry as a case study. Proceedings of the National Academy of Sciences, USA 103: 10140-10145.

Gratwicke, B.; Lovejoy, T. E.; Wildt, D. E. 2012. Will amphibians croak under the Endangered Species Act? BioScience 62: 197-202.

Gray, M. J.; Miller, D. L.; Hoverman, J. T. 2009. Ecology and pathology of amphibian ranaviruses. Diseases of Aquatic Organisms 87: 243-266.

Gutzwiller, K. J.; Flather, C. H. 2011. Wetland features and landscape context predict the risk of wetland habitat loss. Ecological Applications 21: 968-982.

Haufler, J. B., ed. 2005. Fish and wildlife benefits of Farm Bill Conservation Programs: 2000-2005 update. Technical Review 05-02. Bethesda, MD: The Wildlife Society.

Hecnar, S. J.; M'Closkey, R. T. 1996. Regional dynamics and the status of amphibians. Ecology 77: 2091-2097.

Hector, A.; Joshi, J.; Lawler, S. P.; Spehn, E. M.; Wilby, A. 2001. Conservation implications of the link between biodiversity and ecosystem functioning. Oecologia 129: 624-628.

Herrick, J. E.; Lessard, V. C.; Spaeth, K. E.; Shaver, P. L.; Dayton, R. S.; Pyke, D. A., et al. 2010. National ecosystem assessments supported by scientific and local knowledge. Frontiers in Ecology and the Environment 8: 403-408.

Hof, C.; Araújo, M. B.; Jetz, W.; Rahbek, C. 2011. Additive threats from pathogens, climate and land-use change for global amphibian diversity. Nature 480: 516-519.

Hoffmann, M.; Hilton-Taylor, C.; Angulo, A.; Bohm, M.; Brooks, T. M.; Butchart, S. H., et al. 2010. The impact of conservation on the status of the world's vertebrates. Science 330: 1503-1509.

Houlahan, J. E.; Findlay, C. S.; Schmidt, B. R.; Meyer, A.; Kuzmin, S. L. 2000. Quantitative evidence for global amphibian population declines. Nature 404: 752-755.

Hurley, M. A.; Unsworth, J. W.; Zager, P.; Hebblewhite, M.; Garton, E. O.; Montgomery, D. M., et al. 2011. Demographic response of mule deer to experimental reduction of coyotes and mountain lions in southeastern Idaho. Wildlife Monographs 178: 1-33.

Hurley, P. M.; Webster, C. R.; Flaspohler, D. J.; Parker, G. R. 2012. Untangling the landscape of deer overabundance: Reserve size versus landscape context in the agricultural Midwest. Biological Conservation 146: 62-71.

Huston, M. A. 2005. The three phases of land-use change: implications for biodiversity. Ecological Applications 15: 1864-1878.

IUCN. 2011. The IUCN red list of threatened species. Available: http://www.iucnredlist.org/initiatives/amphibians/analysis/geographic-patterns.

Jenkins, M.; Scherr, S. J.; Inbar, M. 2004. Markets for biodiversity services – potential roles and challenges. Environment 46: 32-42.

Johns, D. 2010. The international year of biodiversity – from talk to action. Conservation Biology 24: 338-340.

Kareiva, P.; Marvier, M. 2011. Conservation science: balancing the needs of people and nature. Geenwood Village, CO: Roberts and Company. 543 p.

Kelley, J. R. 2002. American woodcock population status, 2002. Laurel, MD: U.S. Department of the Interior, Fish and Wildlife Service. 16 p.

Kelley, J. R. 2003. American woodcock population status, 2003. Laurel, MD: U.S. Department of the Interior, Fish and Wildlife Service. 20 p.

Kelley, J. R. 2004. American woodcock population status, 2004. Laurel, Maryland: U.S. Department of the Interior, Fish and Wildlife Service. 15 p.

Kelley, J. R.; Rau, R. D. 2005. American woodcock population status, 2005. Laurel, MD: U.S. Department of the Interior, Fish and Wildlife Service. 15 p.

Kelley, J. R.; Rau, R. D. 2006. American woodcock population status, 2006. Laurel, MD: U.S. Department of the Interior, Fish and Wildlife Service. 15 p.

Kelley, J. R.; Rau, R. D.; Parker, K. 2007. American woodcock population status, 2007. Laurel, MD: U.S. Department of the Interior, Fish and Wildlife Service. 17 p.

Keppie, D. M.; Whiting, R. M. 1994. American woodcock (Scolopax minor). In: Poole, A., ed. Birds of North America. Ithaca, NY: Cornell Lab of Ornithology

Kiesecker, J. M. 2011. Global stressors and the global decline of amphibians: tipping the stress immunocometency axis. Ecological Research 26: 897-908.

Klenner, W.; Arsenault, A. 2009. Ponderosa pine mortality during a severe bark beetle (Coleoptera: Curculionidae, Scolytinae) outbreak in southern British Columbia and implications for wildlife habitat management. Forest Ecology and Management 258: S5-S14.

Knapp, S. 2011. Rarity, species richness, and the threat of extinction – are plants the same as animals? Public Library of Science Biology 9(5): e1001067.

Knick, S. T.; Dobkin, D. S.; Rotenberry, J. T.; Schroeder, M. A.; Vander Haegen, W. M.; van Riper, C. 2003. Teetering on the edge or too late? Conservation and research issues for avifauna of sagebrush habitats. Condor 105: 611-634.

Kremen, C.; Williams, N. M.; Aizen, M. A.; Gemmill-Herren, B.; LeBuhn, G.; Minckley, R., et al. 2007. Pollination and other ecosystem services produced by mobile organisms: a conceptual framework for the effects of land-use change. Ecology Letters 10: 299-314.

Kunz, T. H.; de Torrez, E. B.; Bauer, D.; Lobova, T.; Fleming, T. H. 2011. Ecosystem services provided by bats. Annals of the New York Academy of Sciences 1223: 1-38.

Laband, D. N.; Neiswiadomy, M. 2006. Factors affecting species' risk of extinction: an empirical analysis of ESA and NatureServe listings. Contemporary Economic Policy 24: 160-171.

Lawler, J. J.; Shafer, S. L.; White, D.; Kareiva, P.; Maurer, E. P.; Blaustein, A. R., et al. 2009. Projected climate-induced faunal change in the Western Hemisphere. Ecology 90: 588-597.

Leibowitz, S. G. 2003. Isolated wetlands and their functions: an ecological perspective. Wetlands 23: 517-531.

Leidner, A. K.; Neel, M. C. 2011. Taxonomic and geographic patterns of decline for threatened and endangered species in the United States. Conservation Biology 25: 716-725.

Lepczyk, C. A.; Flather, C. H.; Radeloff, V. C.; Pidgeon, A. M.; Hammer, R. B.; Liu, J. G. 2008. Human impacts on regional avian diversity and abundance. Conservation Biology 22: 405-416.

Levi, T.; Kilpatrick, A. M.; Mangel, M.; Wilmers, C. C. 2012. Deer, predators, and the emergence of Lyme disease. Proceedings of the National Academy of Sciences, USA 109: 10942-10947.

Levin, P. S.; Levin, D. A. 2002. The real biodiversty crisis. American Scientist 90: 6-8.

Levy, S. 2006. A plague of deer. Bioscience 56: 718-721.

Link, W. A.; Sauer, J. R. 1994. Estimating equations estimates of trends. Bird Populations 2: 23-32.

Loftus, A. J.; Flather, C. H. 2012. Fish and other aquatic resource trends in the United States: a technical document supporting the Forest Service 2010 RPA assessment. Gen. Tech. Rep. RMRS-GTR-283. Fort Collins, CO: U.S. Department of Agriculture, Forest Service, Rocky Mountain Research Station. 81 p.

Long, L. E.; Saylor, L. S.; Soule, M. E. 1995. A pH/UV-B synergism in amphibians. Conservation Biology 9: 1301-1303.

Lorch, J. M.; Meteyer, C. U.; Behr, M. J.; Boyles, J. G.; Cryan, P. M.; Hicks, A. C., et al. 2011. Experimental infection of bats with Geomyces destructans causes white-nose syndrome. Nature 480: 376-378.

Loreau, M.; Naeem, S.; Inchausti, P.; Bengtsson, J.; Grime, J. P.; Hector, A., et al. 2001. Biodiversity and ecosystem functioning: current knowledge and future challenges. Science 294: 804-808.

Losey, J. E.; Vaughan, M. 2006. The economic value of ecological services provided by insects. Bioscience 56: 311-323.

Mason, R.; Carpenter, L. H.; Cox, M.; Devos, J. C.; Fairchild, J.; Freddy, D. J., et al. 2006. A case for standardized ungulate surveys and data management in the western United States. Wildlife Society Bulletin 34: 1238-1242.

Master, L. L. 1991. Assessing threats and setting priorities for conservation. Conservation Biology 5: 559-563.

Master, L. L.; Stein, B. A.; Kutner, L. S.; Hammerson, G. A. 2000. Vanishing assests: conservation status of U.S. species. In: Stein, B. A.; Kutner, L. S.; Adams, J. S., eds. Percious heritage: the status of biodiversity in the United States. New York, NY: Oxford University Press: 93-118.

Mehlman, D. W.; Rosenberg, K. V.; Wells, J. V.; Robertson, B. 2004. A comparison of North American avian conservation priority ranking systems. Biological Conservation 120: 383-390.

Mendelson, J. R.; Lips, K. R.; Gagliardo, R. W.; Rabb, G. B.; Collins, J. P.; Diffendorfer, J. E., et al. 2006. Biodiversity - confronting amphibian declines and extinctions. Science 313: 48-48.

Menu, S.; Gauthier, G.; Reed, A. 2002. Changes in survival rates and population dynamics of greater snow geese over a 30-year period: implications for hunting regulations. Journal of Applied Ecology 39: 91-102.

Millennium Ecosystem Assessment. 2005. Ecosystems and human well-being: current state and trends, Volume 1. Washington, DC: Island Press. 917 p.

Mirarchi, R.E. 2001. Mourning dove. In: Dickson, J. G., ed. Wildlife of southern forests: habitat and management. Blaine, WA: Hancock House Publishers: 156-166.

Mockrin, M. H.; Aiken, R. A.; Flather, C. H. 2012. Wildlife-associated recreation trends in the United States: a technical document supporting the Forest Service 2010 RPA assessment. Gen. Tech. Rep. RMRS-GTR-293. Fort Collins, CO: U.S. Department of Agriculture, Forest Service, Rocky Mountain Research Station. 47 p.

Moon, J. A.; Haukos, D. A.; Smith, L. M. 2007. Declining body condition of northern pintails wintering in the Playa Lakes Region. Journal of Wildlife Management 71: 218-221.

Mooney, H.; Mace, G. 2009. Biodiversity policy challenges. Science 325: 1474-1474.

Morse, R. A.; Calderone, N. W. 2000. The value of honey bees as pollinators of U.S. crops in 2000. Bee Culture 128: 1-15.

Mule Deer Working Group. 2004. North American mule deer conservation plan: Western Association of Fish and Wildlife Agencies. http://fishandgame.idaho.gov/public/wildlife/muleDeerInitiative/planWAFWA.pdf [accessed 13 September 2011]

Murray, K. A.; Retallick, R. W. R.; Puschendorf, R.; Skerratt, L. F.; Rosauer, D.; McCallum, H. I., et al. 2011. Assessing spatial patterns of disease risk to biodiversity: implications for the management of the amphibian pathogen, Batrachochytrium dendrobatidis. Journal of Applied Ecology 48: 163-173.

Naeem, S.; Duffy, J. E.; Zavaleta, E. 2012. The functions of biological diversity in an age of extinction. Science 336: 1401-1406.

National Research Council. 1992. Conserving biodiversity: a research agenda for development agencies. Washington, DC: National Academy Press. 127 p.

National Research Council. 2007. Status of pollinators in North America. Washington, DC: The National Academies Press. 307 p.

NatureServe. 2010. NatureServe Central Databases. Accessed – 10/13/2010. NatureServe, Arlington, VA. (Metadata on file with Michael S. Knowles, Rocky Mountain Research Station, Fort Collins, CO).

NatureServe. 2011. NatureServe Central Databases. Accessed – 05/08/2011. NatureServe, Arlington, VA. (Metadata on file with Michael S. Knowles, Rocky Mountain Research Station, Fort Collins, CO).

Naugle, D. E.; Doherty, K. E.; Walker, B. L.; Holloran, M. J.; Copeland, H. E. 2011. Energy development and greater sage-grouse. Studies in Avian Biology 38: 489-502.

Nakagawa, S. 2004. A farewell to Bonferroni: the problems of low statistical power and publication bias. Behavioral Ecology 15: 1044-1045.

Newson, S. E.; Johnston, A.; Renwick, A. R.; Baillie, S. R.; Fuller, R. J. 2012. Modelling large-scale relationships between changes in woodland deer and bird populations. Journal of Applied Ecology 49: 278-286.

Nichols, J. D.; Johnson, F. A.; Williams, B. K. 1995. Managing North American waterfowl in the face of uncertainty. Annual Review of Ecology and Systematics 26: 177-199.

Nichols, J. D.; Runge, M. C.; Johnson, F. A.; Williams, B. K. 2007. Adaptive harvest management of North American waterfowl populations: a brief history and future prospects. Journal of Ornithology 148: S343-S349.

Nielson, R. M.; McDonald, L. L.; Sullivan, J. P.; Burgess, C.; Johnson, D. S.; Johnson, D. H., et al. 2008. Estimating the response of Ring-necked Pheasants (*Phasianus colchicus*) to the Conservation Reserve Program. Auk 125: 434-444.

O'Gara, B.W.; Morrison, B. 2004. Managing the harvest. In: O'Gara, B.W.; Yoakum, J.D., eds. Pronghorn ecology and management. Boulder, CO: University Press of Colorado: 673-704.

O'Shea, T. J.; Bogan, M. A.; Ellison, L. E. 2003. Monitoring trends in bat populations of the United States and territories: status of the science and recommendations for the future. Wildlife Society Bulletin 31: 16-29.

Ohmer, M. E.; Bishop, P. J. 2011. Citation rate and perceived subject bias in the amphibian-decline literature. Conservation Biology 25: 195-199.

Ollerton, J.; Winfree, R.; Tarrant, S. 2011. How many flowering plants are pollinated by animals? Oikos 120: 321-326.

Organ, J. F.; Decker, T.; Langlois, S.; Mirick, P. G. 2001. Trapping and furbearer management in North American wildlife conservation. Coordinated by the Massachusetts Division of Fisheries and Wildlife and the U.S. Fish and Wildilfe Service, Division of Federal Aid, Northeast Furbearer Resources Technical Committee. 41 p.

Organ, J. F.; Mahoney, S. P.; Geist, V. 2010. Born in the hands of hunters: the North American model of wildlife conservation. The Wildlife Professional 4(3): 22-27.

Padding, P. I.; Richkus, K. D.; Moore, M. T.; Martin, E. M.; Williams, S. S.; Spriggs, H. L. 2005. Migratory bird hunting activity and harvest during the 2003 and 2004 hunting seasons, preliminary estimates. Washington, DC: U.S. Department of the Interior, Fish and Wildlife Service. 67 p.

Pascual, U.; Perrings, C. 2007. Developing incentives and economic mechanisms for *in situ* biodiversity conservation in agricultural landscapes. Agriculture Ecosystems & Environment 121: 256-268.

Pechmann, J. H. K.; Scott, D. E.; Semlitsch, R. D.; Caldwell, J. P.; Vitt, L. J.; Gibbons, J. W. 1991. Declining amphibian populations – the problem of separating human impacts from natural fluctuations. Science 253: 892-895.

Pechmann, J. H. K.; Wilbur, H. M. 1994. Putting declining amphibian populations in perspective - natural fluctuations and human impacts. Herpetologica 50: 65-84.

Perneger, T. V. 1998. What's wrong with Bonferroni adjustments. BMJ 316: 1236-1238.

Peterjohn, B. G.; Sauer, J. R. 1993. North American Breeding Bird Survey annual summary 1990 – 1991. Bird Populations 1: 1-15.

Petranka, J. W.; Eldridge, M. E.; Haley, K. E. 1993. Effects of timer harvesting on southern Appalachian salamanders. Conservation Biology 7: 363-377.

Pidgeon, A. M.; Radeloff, V. C.; Flather, C. H.; Lepczyk, C. A.; Clayton, M. K.; Hawbaker, T. J., et al. 2007. Associations of forest bird species richness with housing and landscape patterns across the USA. Ecological Applications 17: 1989-2010.

Pimentel, D.; Wilson, C.; McCullum, C.; Huang, R.; Dwen, P.; Flack, J., et al. 1997. Economic and environmental benefits of biodiversity. BioScience 47: 747-757.

Podruzny, K. M.; Devries, J. H.; Armstrong, L. M.; Rotella, J. J. 2002. Long-term response of northern pintails to changes in wetlands and agriculture in the Canadian Prairie Pothole Region. Journal of Wildlife Management 66: 993-1010.

Potts, S. G.; Biesmeijer, J. C.; Kremen, C.; Neumann, P.; Schweiger, O.; Kunin, W. E. 2010. Global pollinator declines: trends, impacts and drivers. Trends in Ecology & Evolution 25: 345-353.

Prendergast, J. R.; Quinn, R. M.; Lawton, J. H.; Eversham, B. C.; Gibbons, D. W. 1993. Rare species, the coincidence of diversity hotspots and conservation strategies. Nature 365: 335-337.

Pyle, R.; Bentzien, M.; Opler, P. 1981. Insect conservation. Annual Review of Entomology 26: 233-258.

Radeloff, V. C.; Stewart, S. I.; Hawbaker, T. J.; Gimmi, U.; Pidgeon, A. M.; Flather, C. H., et al. 2010. Housing growth in and near United States protected areas limits their conservation value. Proceedings of the National Academy of Sciences, USA 107: 940-945.

Raftovich, R. V.; Wilkins, K. A.; Richkus, K. D.; Williams, S. S.; Spriggs, H. L. 2009. Migratory bird hunting activity and harvest during the 2007 and 2008 hunting seasons. Laurel, MD: U.S. Department of the Interior, Fish and Wildlife Service. 63 p.

Raftovich, R. V.; Wilkins, K. A.; Richkus, K. D.; Williams, S. S.; Spriggs, H. L. 2010. Migratory bird hunting activity and harvest during the 2008 and 2009 hunting seasons. Laurel, MD: U.S. Department of the Interior, Fish and Wildlife Service. 63 p.

Raithel, C. J.; Paton, P. W. C.; Pooler, P. S.; Golet, F. C. 2011. Assessing long-term population trends of wood frogs using egg-mass counts. Journal of Herpetology 45: 23-27.

Rands, M. R.; Adams, W. M.; Bennun, L.; Butchart, S. H.; Clements, A.; Coomes, D., et al. 2010. Biodiversity conservation: challenges beyond 2010. Science 329: 1298-1303.

Rapport, D. J.; Regier, H. A.; Hutchinson, T. C. 1985. Ecosystem behavior under stress. American Naturalist 125: 617-640.

Raudsepp-Hearne, C.; Capistrano, D. 2010. The Millennium Ecosystem Assessment: a multi-scale assessment for global stakeholders. In: Lawrence, A., ed. Taking stock of nature: participatory biodiversity assessment for policy, planning and practice. Cambrige, UK: Cambridge University Press: 49-68.

Reed, J. M.; Blaustein, A. R. 1995. Assessment of nondeclining amphibian populations using power analysis. Conservation Biology 9: 1299-1300.

Reeves, J. M.; Tomlinson, R. E.; Bartonek, J. C. 1993. Population characteristics and trends in the western management unit. In: Baskett, T.S.; Sayre, M.W.; Tomlinson, R.E.; Mirarchi, R.E., eds. Ecology and management of the mourning dove. Harrisburg, PA: Stackpole Books: 341-376.

Reichard, J. D.; Kunz, T. H. 2009. White-nose syndrome inflicts lasting injuries to the wings of little brown myotis (*Myotis lucifugus*). Acta Chiropterologica 11: 457-464.

Reynolds, R. E.; Shaffer, T. L.; Renner, R. W.; Newton, W. E.; Batt, B. D. J. 2001. Impact of the conservation reserve program on duck recruitment in the US Prairie Pothole Region. Journal of Wildlife Management 65: 765-780.

Ricketts, T. H.; Dinerstein, E.; Olson, D. M.; Loucks, C. 1999. Who's where in North America? BioScience 49: 369-381.

Riitters, K. 2011. Spatial patterns of land cover in the United States: a technical document supporting the Forest Service 2010 RPA assessement. Gen. Tech. Rep. SRS-136. Asheville, NC: U.S. Department of Agriculture, Forest Service, Southern Research Station. 64 p.

Robbins, C. S.; Bystrak, D.; Geissler, P. H. 1986. The Breeding Bird Survey: its first fifteen years, 1965-1979. Resource Publication 157. Washington, DC: U.S. Department of the Interior, Fish and Wildlife Service. 196 p.

Robles, M. D.; Flather, C. H.; Stein, S. M.; Nelson, M. D.; Cutko, A. 2008. The geography of private forests that support at-risk species in the conterminous United States. Frontiers in Ecology and the Environment 6: 301-307.

Rohr, J. R.; Halstead, N. T.; Raffel, T. R. 2011. Modelling the future distribution of the amphibian chytrid fungus: the influence of climate and human-associated factors. Journal of Applied Ecology 48: 174-176.

Saab, V. A.; Powell, H. D. 2005. Fire and avian ecology in North America: process influencing pattern. Studies in Avian Biology 30: 1-13.

Sala, O. E.; Chapin, F. S.; Armesto, J. J.; Berlow, E.; Bloomfield, J.; Dirzo, R., et al. 2000. Biodiversity – global biodiversity scenarios for the year 2100. Science 287: 1770-1774.

Sanders, T. A.; Parker, K. 2010. Mourning dove population status, 2010. Washington, DC: U.S. Department of the Interior, Fish and Wildlife Service, Division of Migratory Bird Management. 28 p.

Sauer, J. R.; Link, W. A. 2002. Hierarchical modeling of population stability and species group attributes from survey data. Ecology 86: 1743-1751.

Sawyer, H.; Nielson, R. M.; Lindzey, F.; McDonald, L. L. 2006. Winter habitat selection of mule deer before and during development of a natural gas field. Journal of Wildlife Management 70: 396-403.

Schimel, D. 2011. The era of continental-scale ecology. Frontiers in Ecology and the Environment 9: 311.

Shifley, S. R. In press. Criterion 1: Conservation biological diversity. Indicator 6: Status of *in situ* and *ex situ* efforts focused on conservation of species diversity. In: Data report: a supplement to the national report on sustainable forests–2010. FS-000. Washington, DC: U.S. Department of Agriculture, Forest Service.

Sibley, D. 2000. The Sibley guide to birds. New York, NY: Alfred A. Knopf. 544 p.

Southwick, R.; Woolley, A.; Leonard, D.; Rushton, S. 2005. Potential costs of losing hunting and trapping as wildlife management methods. Animal Use Issues Committee. Washington, DC: International Association of Fish and Wildlife Agencies. 52 p.

Steffan-Dewenter, I.; Potts, S. G.; Packer, L. 2005. Pollinator diversity and crop pollination services are at risk. Trends in Ecology & Evolution 20: 651-652.

Stein, B. A.; Adams, J. S.; Master, L. L.; Morse, L. E.; Hammerson, G. A. 2000a. A remarkable array: species diversity in the United States. In: Stein, B. A.; Kutner, L. S.; Adams, J. S., eds. Precious heritage: the status of biodiversity in the United States. Oxford, UK: Oxford University Press: 55-92.

Stein, B. A.; Kutner, L. S.; Hammerson, G. A.; Master, L. L.; Morse, L. E. 2000b. State of the states: geographic patterns of diversity, rarity, and endemism. In: Stein, B. A.; Kutner, L. S.; Adams, J. S., eds. Precious heritage: the status of biodiversity in the United States. Oxford, UK: Oxford University Press: 119-157.

Stein, B. A.; Scott, C.; Benton, N. 2008. Federal lands and endangered species: the role of military and other federal lands in sustaining biodiversity. Bioscience 58: 339-347.

Stein, S. M.; McRoberts, R. E.; Nelson, M. D.; Mahal, L.; Flather, C. H.; Alig, R. J., et al. 2010. Private forest habitat for at-risk species: where is it and where might it be changing? Journal of Forestry 108: 61-70.

Stokstad, E. 2010. Despite progress, biodiversity declines. Science 329: 1272-1273.

Stuart, S. N.; Chanson, J. S.; Cox, N. A.; Young, B. E.; Rodrigues, A. S. L.; Fischman, D. L., et al. 2004. Status and trends of amphibian declines and extinctions worldwide. Science 306: 1783-1786.

Thomas, J. W. 1990. Wildlife. In: Samson, R. N.; Hair, D., eds. Natural resources for the 21st century. Washington, DC: Island Press: 175-204.

Tiner, R. W. 2003. Geographically isolated wetlands of the United States. Wetlands 23: 494-516.

Tomlison, R.E.; Dunks, J.H. 1993. Population characteristics and trends in the central management unit. In: Baskett, T.S.; Sayre, M.W.; Tomlinson, R.E.; Mirarchi, R.E., eds. Ecology and management of the mourning dove. Harrisburg, PA: Stackpole Books: 305-340.

U.S. Census Bureau. 2001. Census 2000 summary file 1. Washington, DC: U.S. Census Bureau.

U.S. Geological Survey. 2007. Strategic plan for the North American Breeding Bird Survey: 2006–2010. Circular 1307. Washington, DC: U.S. Department of the Interior, U.S. Geological Survey. 19 p.

Unsworth, J. W.; Pac, D. F.; White, G. C.; Bartmann, R. M. 1999. Mule deer survival in Colorado, Idaho, and Montana. Journal of Wildlife Management 63: 315-326.

USDA, Forest Service. 1981. An assessment of the forest and range land situation in the United States. Forest Resources Report 22. Washington, DC: U.S. Department of Agriculture, U.S. Government Printing Office. 352 p.

USDA, Forest Service. 2011. National report on sustainable forests–2010. FS-979. Washington, DC: U.S. Department of Agriculture, Forest Service.

USDA, Forest Service. 2012a. Future of America's forests and rangelands: Forest Service 2010 Resources Planning Act Assessment. Gen. Tech. Rep. WO-87. Washington, D.C.: U.S. Department of Agriculture, Forest Service. 198 p.

USDA, Forest Service. 2012b. Future scenarios: a technical document supporting the Forest Service 2010 RPA Assessment. Gen. Tech. Rep. RMRS-GTR-272. Fort Collins, CO: U.S. Department of Agriculture, Forest Service, Rocky Mountain Research Station. 34 p.

USDI, Fish and Wildlife Service. 1996. Endangered and threatened wildlife and plants; Review of plan and animal taxa that are candidates for listing as endangered or threatened species. Federal Register 61: 7596-7613.

USDI, Fish and Wildlife Service. 2006a. Migratory bird hunting activity and harvest during the 1999 and 2000 hunting seasons – final report. Washington, DC: U.S. Department of the Interior, Fish and Wildlife Service. 92 p.

USDI, Fish and Wildlife Service. 2006b. Migratory bird hunting activity and harvest during the 2004 and 2005 hunting seasons: preliminary estimates. Washington, DC: U.S. Department of the Interior, Fish and Wildlife Service. 63 p.

USDI, Fish and Wildlife Service. 2007a. Migratory bird hunting activity and harvest during the 2001 and 2002 hunting seasons – final report. Washington, DC: U.S. Department of the Interior, Fish and Wildlife Service. 92 p.

USDI, Fish and Wildlife Service. 2007b. Migratory bird hunting activity and harvest during the 2005 and 2006 hunting seasons: preliminary estimates. Wasington, DC: U.S. Department of the Interior, Fish and Wildlife Service. 62 p.

USDI, Fish and Wildlife Service. 2010. Waterfowl population status report, 2010. Washington, DC: U.S. Department of the Interior, Fish and Wildlife Service. 79 p.

USDI, Fish and Wildlife Service. 2011. A national plan for assisting states, federal agencies, and tribes in managing white-nose syndrome in bats. Hadley, MA: U.S. Department of the Interior, Fish and Wildlife Service. 17 p.

USDI, Fish and Wildlife Service. 2012. White-nose syndrome confirmed in federally endangered gray bats. News Release. 29 May 2012. Contacts: A. Froschauer, and P. McKenzie.

USDI, Fish and Wildlife Service; Environment Canada, Canadian Wildlife Service; SEDESOL, Mexico. 1994. North American waterfowl management plan, 1994 update. Expanding the commitment. Washington, DC: U.S. Government Printing Office. 30 p.

Vance, M. D.; Fahrig, L.; Flather, C. H. 2003. Effect of reproductive rate on minimum habitat requirements of forest-breeding birds. Ecology 84: 2643-2653.

Vial, J. L.; Saylor, L. 1993. The status of amphibian populations: a compilation and analysis. Working document No. 1. IUCN, Species Survival Commission. 98 p.

Vitousek, P. M.; Mooney, H. A.; Lubchenco, J.; Melillo, J. M. 1997. Human domination of earth's ecosystems. Science 277: 494-499.

Vogelmann, J. E.; Howard, S. M.; Yang, L. M.; Larson, C. R.; Wylie, B. K.; Van Driel, N. 2001. Completion of the 1990s national land cover data set for the conterminous United States from landsat thematic mapper data and ancillary data sources. Photogrammetric Engineering and Remote Sensing 67: 650-662.

Wake, D. B. 2012. Facing extinction in real time. Science 335: 1052-1053.

Walther, G. R.; Post, E.; Convey, P.; Menzel, A.; Parmesan, C.; Beebee, T. J. C., et al. 2002. Ecological responses to recent climate change. Nature 416: 389-395.

Warnecke, L.; Turner, J. M.; Bollinger, T. K.; Lorch, J. M.; Misra, V.; Cryan, P. M., et al. 2012. Inoculation of bats with European Geomyces destructans supports the novel pathogen hypothesis for the origin of white-nose syndrome. Proceedings of the National Academy of Sciences, USA 109: 6999-7003.

Wear, D. N. 2011. Forecasts of county-level land uses under three future scenarios: a technical document supporting the Forest Service 2010 RPA Assessment. Gen. Tech. Rep. SRS-141. Ashville, NC: U.S. Department of Agriculture, Forest Service, Southern Research Station. 41 p.

Weir, L. A.; Mossman, M. J. 2005. North American Amphibian Monitoring Program (NAAMP). In: Lannoo, M., ed. Amphibian declines: the conservation status of United States species. Berkeley, CA: University of California Press: 307-313.

Weir, L. A.; Royle, J. A.; Nanjappa, P.; Jung, R. E. 2005. Modeling anuran detection and site occupancy on North American Amphibian Monitoring Program (NAAMP) routes in Maryland. Journal of Herpetology 39: 627-639.

Weir, L.; Fiske, I. J.; Royle, J. A. 2009. Trends in anuran occupancy from northeastern states of the North American Amphibian Monitoring Program. Herpetological Conservation and Biology 4: 389-402.

Wiens, D.; Slaton, M. R. 2012. The mechanism of background extinction. Biological Journal of the Linnean Society 105: 255-268.

Williams, B. K.; Nichols, J. D.; Conroy, M. J. 2002. Analysis and management of animal populations. San Diego, CA: Academic Press. 817 p.

Williams, C. K.; Guthery, F. S.; Applegate, R. D.; Peterson, M. J. 2004. The northern bob-white decline: scaling our management for the twenty-first century. Wildlife Society Bulletin 32: 861-869.

Wissinger, S. A.; Whiteman, H. H. 1992. Fluctuation in a Rocky Mountain population of salamanders – anthropogenic acidification or natural variations? Journal of Herpetology 26: 377-391.

Woodwell, G. M. 2010. The biodiversity blunder. BioScience 60: 870-871.

Zinn, J. A.; Copeland, C. 2006. Wetlands: an overview. CRS Report RL33483. Washington, D.C.: Congressional Research Service. 20 p.

Appendix A: Glossary of Terms Used in the Text

amphibian – a cold-blooded, smooth-skinned vertebrate of the class Amphibia, such as a frog or salamander, that characteristically hatches as an aquatic larva with gills. The larva then transforms into an adult having air-breathing lungs.

anthropogenic – of, relating to, or resulting from the influence of human beings on nature.

aquatic – living in or on water for all or a substantial part of the life span, generally restricted to fresh water or inland waters.

at-risk – species that are critically imperiled, imperiled, or vulnerable according to NatureServe's conservation ranking criteria.

bees – a monophyletic lineage within the superfamily Apoidea.

big game – primarily large mammal species that are taken for sport or subsistence; also includes wild turkey by convention of many state agencies.

bumble bees – species of the genus *Bombus*.

candidate species – a species for which the U.S. Fish and Wildlife Service has sufficient information on file to support proposals to list the species as threatened or endangered, but for which preparation and publication of a listing proposal is precluded by other listing activities.

canopy nesting – a species that nests in a tree's uppermost layer.

cavity nesting – a species that excavates its own cavities or uses natural or previously excavated cavities for nesting.

conservation concern – species classified as at-risk, presumed extinct, or possibly extinct.

crustacean – one of the classes of the arthropods, including lobsters and crabs, so called from the crust like shell with which it is covered.

ecoregion – an area defined by its environmental conditions, especially climate, landforms, soil characteristics, and biota.

ecosystem – a system formed by the interaction of a community of organisms with its environment.

ecosystem function – the capacity of natural processes and components to provide goods and services that satisfy human needs, either directly or indirectly.

ecosystem services – the important benefits for human beings that arise from healthily functioning ecosystems.

endangered – a species, including subspecies or distinct population segment, that is in danger of extinction throughout all or a significant portion of its range.

extinct – no longer living or existing.

extinction – the complete disappearance of a species from the earth.

extirpation – the extinction of a population; the complete eradication of a species within a specified area; generally connotes an unnatural cause.

federal trust species – species for which the federal government has primary jurisdiction. Examples are species listed under the Endangered Species Act, migratory birds protected by international treaties, and native plant or wildlife species found on a national wildlife refuge or wetland management district.

feral – existing in a wild or untamed state.

flyway – lanes of individual travel from any particular breeding ground to the winter quarters of the birds that typically use them.

forest bird – a bird species that regularly breeds in forest ecosystems.

frog – any of numerous tailless, aquatic, semi-aquatic, or terrestrial amphibians of the order Anura and especially of the family Ranidae, characteristically having a smooth moist skin, webbed feet, and long hind legs adapted for leaping.

furbearer – mammal species that have traditionally been trapped or harvested primarily for their fur.

grassland habitat – habitat, such as prairie or meadow, on which grass predominates.

ground nesting – a species that builds its nest on or near the ground.

habitat – the place where an organism typically lives and grows; a suite of existing environmental conditions required by an organism for survival and reproduction.

habitat affinity – the relative concentration of a species in a particular habitat, when compared with the relative availability of that habitat across a broader area.

habitat fragmentation – the breaking up of once-contiguous habitat into a complex matrix of spatially isolated habitat patches amid a human-dominated landscape.

hibernacula – hibernation sites in the winter.

hibernation – an energy-conserving lowering of metabolism, respiration, heart rate, and body temperature while the body survives on accumulated fat supplies.

imperiled – endangered, threatened, or species of special concern.

interior nesting – a species that prefers to nest away from habitat edges.

invertebrate – of or pertaining to creatures without a backbone.

landscape – a heterogeneous land area composed of a cluster of interacting ecosystems that is repeated in similar form throughout.

microclimate – the climate of a small, specific place within an area as contrasted with the climate of the entire area.

midstory nesting – a species that nests in the midstory, characterized by the zone beneath the overstory canopy.

migrant species – a species that migrates between its breeding and wintering ranges.

migratory – pertaining to the seasonal movement from breeding grounds to wintering grounds.

mollusk – any invertebrate of the phylum Mollusca, having a soft unsegmented body and often a shell, secreted by a fold of skin.

neotropical migrant – a species that breeds in the United States and winters south of the U.S.–Mexico border; also referred to as a long-distance migrant.

nocturnal – most active at night.

nongame – species that are not consumptively taken for sport, subsistence, or profit.

open cup nesting – a species that utilizes an open cup-shaped nest made with a variety of materials.

open water habitat – habitat that is free from emergent vegetation, artificial obstructions, or tangled masses of underwater vegetation at very shallow depths.

pathogen – a microorganism that makes its host sick.

permanent resident – a species that regularly occurs within a defined range throughout the year.

pollinator – species that carries pollen from one seed plant to another, unwittingly aiding the plant in its reproduction.

population – all the organisms that constitute a specific group or occur in a specified habitat.

population segment – a population or group of populations that is discrete from other populations of the species and significant in relation to the entire species.

predation – a process whereby an organism of one species captures and feeds on another organism of a second species that serves as the prey.

proposed species – species for which a proposed rule to list as either threatened or endangered has been formally published in the Federal Register (pertains to a listing under the Endangered Species Act).

richness – the number of species within a biological community.

salamander – tailed amphibians, cold-blooded, having soft skin that is usually moist and must have a humid if not wet environment.

short-distance migrant – a species that moves short distances (geographic and altitudinal), often in response to local weather conditions.

shrubland habitat – habitat associated with woody plants of relatively low height, having several stems and lacking a single trunk.

small game – small-bodied resident mammals or birds, native or non-native species introduced for recreation opportunities, and hunted recreationally or for subsistence.

species – a fundamental category of taxonomic classification, ranking below a genus or subgenus and consisting of related organisms capable of interbreeding.

species of conservation concern – wildlife species, vertebrate or invertebrate, that shows evidence of population declines.

subspecies – a taxonomic subdivision of a species consisting of an interbreeding, usually geographically isolated population of organisms.

sustainable – capable of being maintained at a steady level without exhausting natural resources or causing severe ecological damage.

synanthropes – a species that tolerates or thrives in habitats associated with human settlement.

taxon/taxa – a taxonomic category or group, such as a phylum, order, family, genus, or species.

temporal – of, relating to, or limited by time.

terrestrial – living or growing on land; not aquatic.

threatened – a species likely to become an endangered species within the foreseeable future throughout all or a significant portion of its range.

toad – any of numerous tailless amphibians chiefly of the family Bufonidae, related to and resembling the frogs but characteristically more terrestrial and having a broader body and rougher, drier skin.

urban habitat – habitat associated with city or town environments.

urbanization – the physical growth of urban areas.

vasculotropic – invades the blood vessels.

vertebrates – members of the subphylum Vertebrata, a primary division of the phylum Chordata, which includes the fishes, amphibians, reptiles, birds, and mammals, all of which are characterized by a segmented spinal column and a distinct well-differentiated head.

waterfowl – wildfowl of the order Anseriformes, especially members of the family Anatidae, which includes ducks, geese, and swans.

wetland habitat – habitat such as swamps, bogs, and marshes where water either covers the soil or is present at or near the surface, particularly in the root zone, for a substantial portion of the year, including the growing season.

wildlife – wild, free-ranging, and undomesticated vertebrate or invertebrate species primarily inhabiting terrestrial ecosystems that may be indigenous or introduced to the United States.

woodland habitat – habitat where trees are the dominant plant form.

Appendix B: Scientific Names of Species and Subspecies Mentioned in the Text

Allen's hummingbird – *Selasphorus sasin*

American black bear – *Ursus americanus*

American black duck – *Anas rubripes*

American wigeon – *Anas americana*

Anna's hummingbird – *Calypte anna*

Barrow's goldeneye – *Bucephala islandica*

Big brown bat – *Eptesicus fuscus*

Black scoter – *Melanitta nigra*

Black-chinned hummingbird – *Archilochus alexandri*

Blue grouse – Dusky grouse and sooty grouse

Blue-winged teal – *Anas discors*

Brant – *Branta bernicla*

Broad-tailed hummingbird – *Selasphorus platycercus*

Bufflehead – *Bucephala albeola*

California quail – *Callipepla californica*

Canada goose – *Branta canadensis*

Canvasback – *Aythya valisineria*

Chukar – *Alectoris chukar*

Common goldeneye – *Bucephala clangula*

Common merganser – *Mergus merganser*

Cottontail – Species of the genus *Sylvilagus*

Dusky Canada goose – *Branta canadensis occidentalis*

Dusky grouse – *Dendragapus obscurus*

Eastern small-footed bat – *Myotis leibii*

Eider – Species of the genera *Somateria* and *Polysticta*

Elk – *Cervus elaphus*

Emperor goose – *Chen canagica*

European honey bee – *Apis mellifera*

Forest grouse – Ruffed grouse, spruce grouse, and blue grouse

Gadwall – *Anas strepera*

Gambel's quail – *Callipepla gambelii*

White-nose syndrome fungus – *Geomyces destructans*

Goldeneye – Common goldeneye and Barrow's goldeneye

Gray bat – *Myotis grisescens*

Gray partridge – *Perdix perdix*

Greater prairie-chicken – *Tympanuchus cupido*

Greater scaup – *Aythya marila*

Greater snow goose – *Chen caerulescens atlantica*

Green-winged teal – *Anas crecca*

Hare – Species of the genus *Lepus*

Hooded merganser – *Lophodytes cucullatus*

Indiana bat – *Myotis sodalis*

Lesser scaup – *Aythya affinis*

Lesser prairie-chicken – *Tympanuchus pallidicinctus*

Lesser snow goose – *Chen caerulescens caerulescens*

Light geese – Snow goose, Ross' goose, lesser snow goose, and greater snow goose

Little brown bat – *Myotis lucifugus*

Long-tailed duck – *Clangula hyemalis*

Mallard – *Anas platyrhynchos*

Merganser – Common merganser, hooded merganser, and red-breasted merganser

Montezuma quail – *Cyrtonyx montezumae*

Mountain quail – *Oreortyx pictus*

Mourning dove – *Zenaida macroura*

Mule deer – *Odocoileus hemionus*

Muskrat – *Ondatra zibethicus*

Northern bobwhite – *Colinus virginianus*

Northern long-eared bat – *Myotis septentrionalis*

Northern pintail – *Anas acuta*

Northern shoveler – *Anas clypeata*

Oahu tree snail – *Achatinella* spp.

Prairie grouse – Greater prairie-chicken, lesser prairie-chicken, sharp-tailed grouse, and sage grouse

Pronghorn – *Antilocapra americana*

Raccoon – *Procyon lotor*

Red squirrel – *Tamiasciurus hudsonicus*

Red-breasted merganser – *Mergus serrator*

Redhead – *Aythya americana*

Ring-necked duck – *Aythya collaris*

Ring-necked pheasant – *Phasianus colchicus*

Ross' goose – *Chen rossii*

Ruby-throated hummingbird – *Archilochus colubris*

Ruddy duck – *Oxyura jamaicensis*

Ruffed grouse – *Bonasa umbellus*

Rufous hummingbird – *Selasphorus rufus*

Sage grouse – *Centrocercus urophasianus* and *C. minimus*

Scaled quail – *Callipepla squamata*

Scaup – Greater scaup, Lesser scaup

Scoter – Black scoter, white-winged scoter, and surf scoter

Sharp-tailed grouse – *Tympanuchus phasianellus*

Snow goose – *Chen caerulescens*

Sooty grouse – *Dendragapus fuliginosus*

Spruce grouse – *Falcipennis canadensis*

Squirrel – Species of the genus *Sciurus* and red squirrel

Surf scoter – *Melanitta perspicillata*

Tricolored bat – *Perimyotis subflavus*

Tundra swan – *Cygnus columbianus*

Western quail – Montezuma quail, scaled quail, Gambel's quail, California quail, and mountain quail

White-fronted goose – *Anser albifrons*

White-tailed deer – *Odocoileus virginianus*

White-winged scoter – *Melanitta fusca*

Wild turkey – *Meleagris gallopavo*

Wood duck – *Aix sponsa*

Woodcock – *Scolopax minor*

Appendix C: County-Level Counts of Species Formally Listed as Threatened or Endangered by Broad Species Groupings

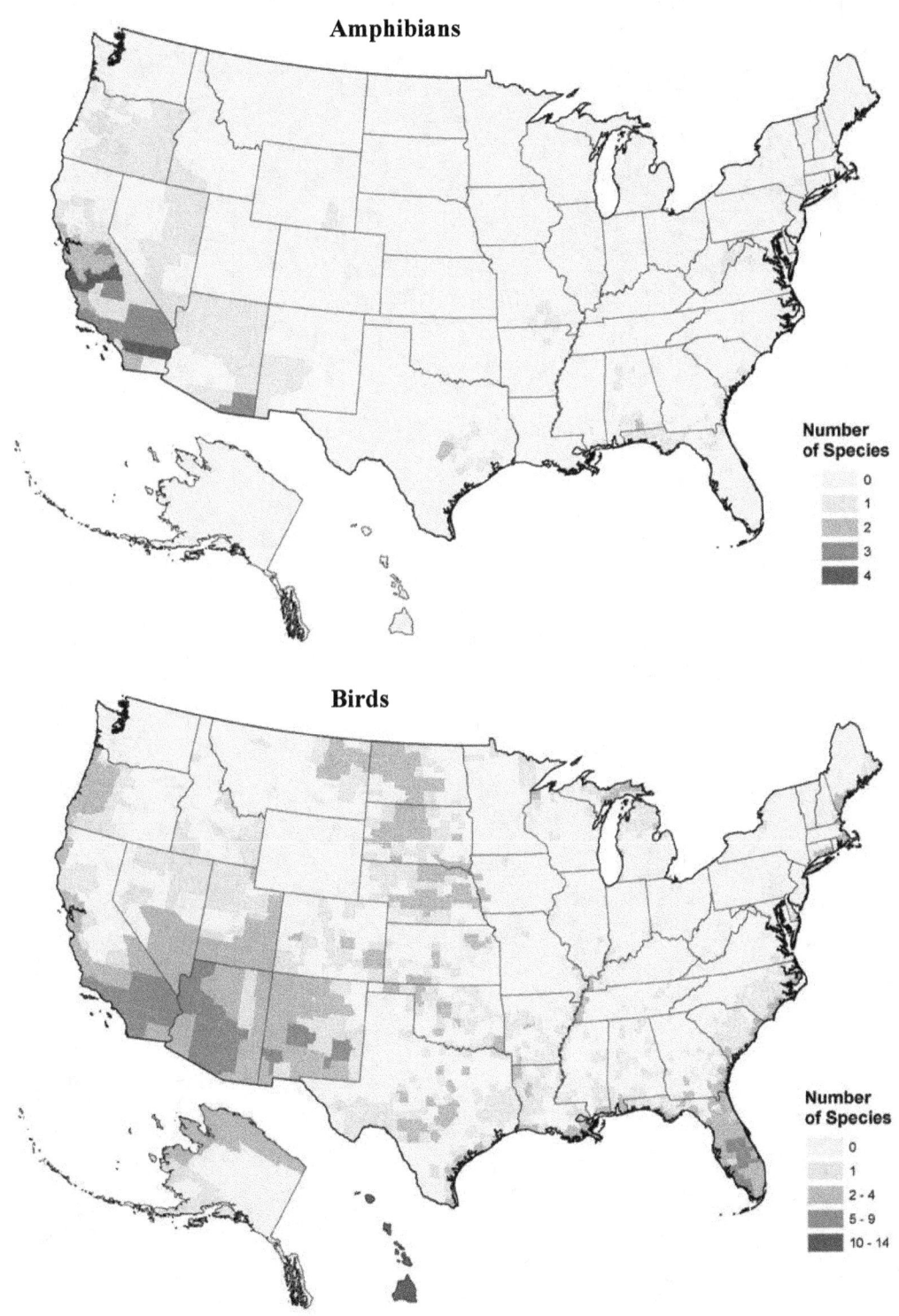

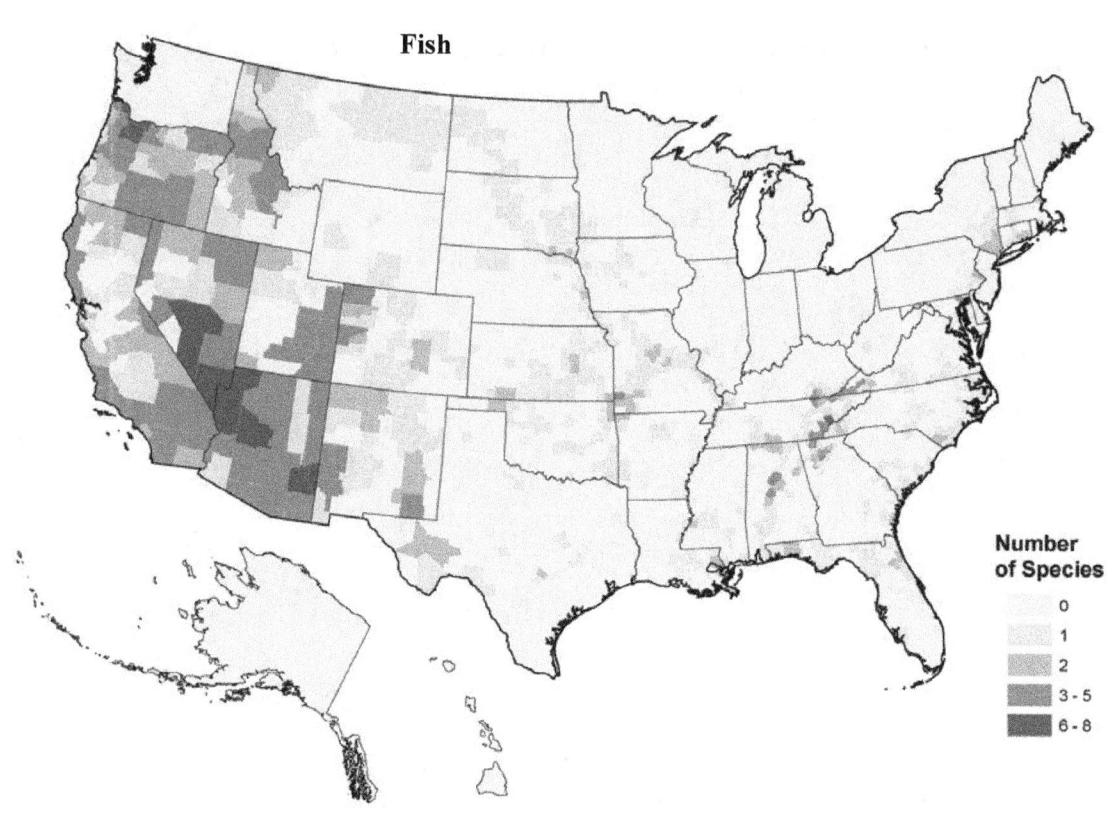

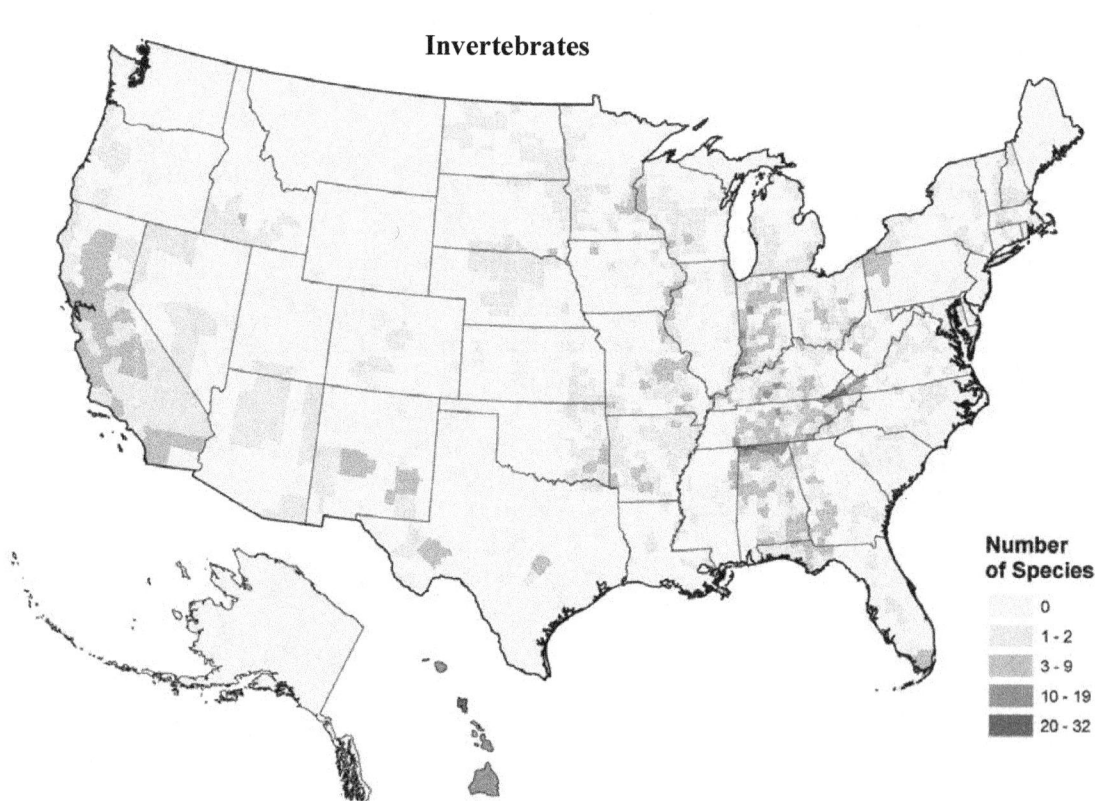

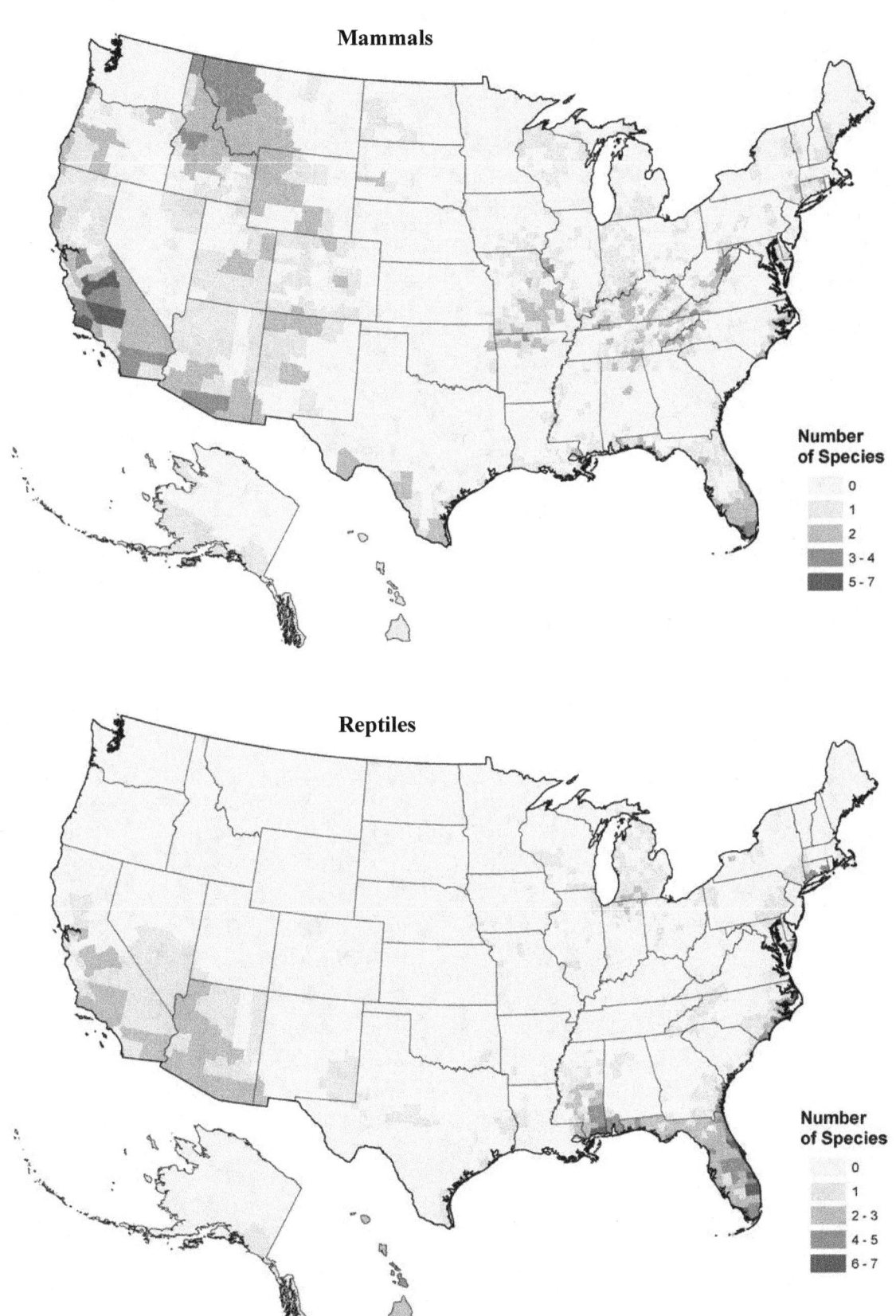

Vascular plants

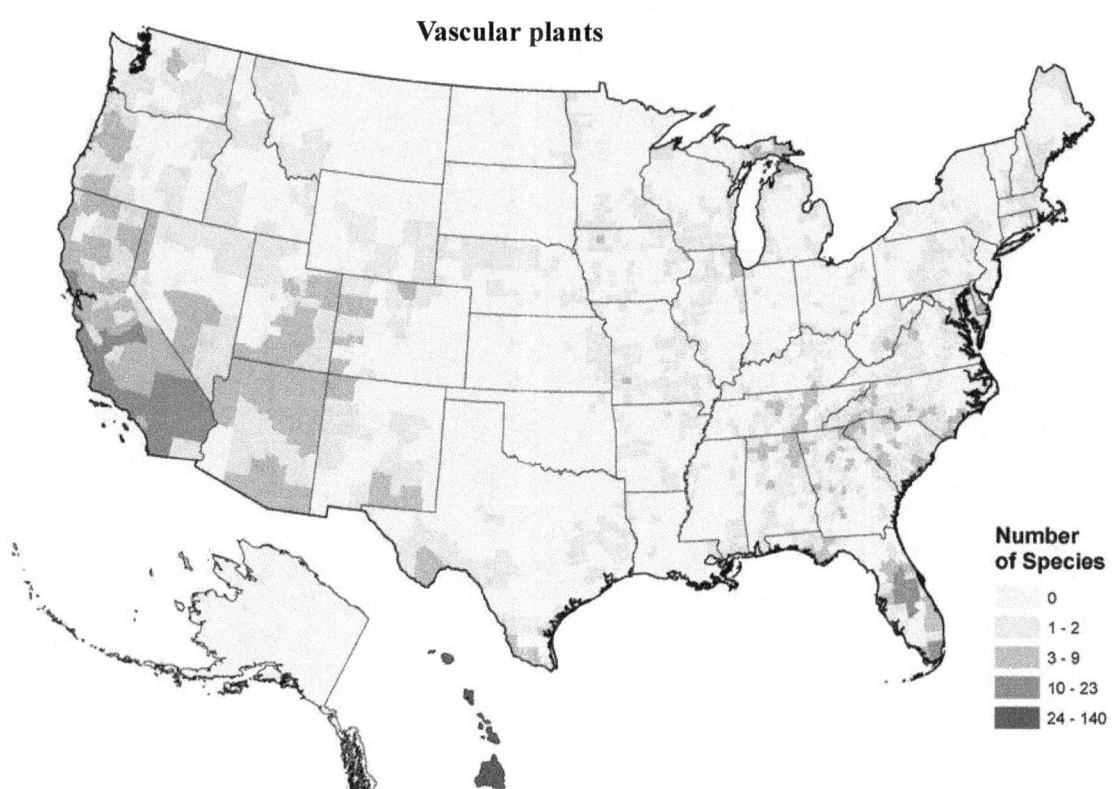

Number
of Species

	0
	1 - 2
	3 - 9
	10 - 23
	24 - 140

USDA
United States Department of Agriculture

Forest Service

RPA

Rocky Mountain Research Station

General Technical Report RMRS-GTR-296

March 2013